Greatest Secrets

of the **Coupon Mom**

by Stephanie Nelson

PRINTED IN THE UNITED STATES OF AMERICA

Cover Design: Jeremy Hunt
Author Photo: Brian Poane

For information regarding Special Editions and special discounts for bulk purchases, please contact: DPL Press, Inc., P.O. Box 2135, Los Angeles, Calif., 90723; Special Sales: 800-550-3502.

Visit us at www.DPLPress.com

First edition published 2005

Library of Congress Cataloging-in-Publication data information available by request from publisher.

ISBN 10   0-9760791-2-7
ISBN 13 978-0-9760791-2-5

1   2   3   4   5   6   7   8   9   10   11   12   13   14   15

Greatest Secrets
of the Coupon Mom

by Stephanie Nelson

With love to Dave ...

the best deal I ever found

Table of Contents

Acknowledgments

The past five years have taught me that to do anything well you need help and support from other people. Thank goodness I had many friends, family members, neighbors, website users, and supporters who were willing to listen, encourage, work on, and pray about the Cut Out Hunger project. I am grateful to every single one of them for helping make this Cut Out Hunger dream a reality.

I owe a special thank you to my mother, Carole King, for patiently listening to me talk about Cut Out Hunger—all the time. Her faith and encouragement carried me along many times. Thank you to my father, Bill Ives, for teaching me the value of being frugal in the first place. And a big thank you goes to my family: my husband, Dave, and sons, David and Christopher. I appreciate your support, patience, love, and understanding as Cut Out Hunger has grown.

I thank the *Good Morning America* team from the bottom of my heart for moving the mountain for me. If it weren't for Lisa Sharkey's willingness to listen, contribute her creative vision, and conceive of the "Coupon Mom" in the first place, none of this would have happened. I will always be grateful to Lisa for taking a chance with me. I also appreciate Maria Licari for her endless patience and kindness—working with her is a true pleasure. Thanks to the creativity and hard work of the *Good Morning America* producers, directors, writers, and anchors, as well as the wonderful support from their viewers, this mom's dream has come true.

Along the way, many people publicly promoted Cut Out Hunger, pushed me to look further, or pulled me along when I couldn't see the way. I am immensely grateful to so many people and will take the risk of naming only a few: Todd Mark, Mary Hunt, Clark Howard, David Gregg; Barbara Duffy and Susan Lenio of North Fulton Charities; Georgia Tech's College of Computing and students Daag Alemayehu, Karl Zipperer, Max Blinder, and Rick Arnett; the students of Timber Ridge Elementary school and their teachers Pat Eddlemon and Stephanie Meyers; volunteers Solange de Bruyn and Mary McCarthy; journalists Bill Liss, Mark Koebrich, Sherri Palmeri, Ellen Kolodziej, Tucker McQueen, Jennifer Brett, Elizabeth Lee, Lisa Rayam, Ric Romero, Kim Nguyen, and Tak Landrock; the Cut Out Hunger team of DeAnn Kelly, Laura Nygaard, Kendra Gagen, and Shayna Adelman; and many who have pitched in, including Toni Hennly, Joe Jackson, Tamara Oliverio, Bill Allen, Kathy Stratton, Heather Reese, Jack McGinnis, the Family Foundations class, Beverly Webb, Meg Mercier, the Aslinger family, Mendes Napoli, and Christine Ives. Thanks to all of you for helping spread the Cut Out Hunger concept. Your efforts made a difference for many people.

Thank you to Mary Hunt, Harold Hunt, Cathy Hollenbeck, and the entire team at DPL Press, Inc., for believing in this book and helping me find a way to share it with far more people.

And last, but certainly not least, I thank God—for allowing this project to grow and continuing to answer our prayers that Cut Out Hunger will continue to help those in need.

Introduction

America knows me as the Coupon Mom. One minute I was discovering ways to save money for my family at the grocery store, and the next I was the Coupon Mom on national television. I now teach people how to save money on their groceries—lots of money every week. Week after week.

It seems like only yesterday, but ten years ago I was working in a corporate job and struggling with the desire to be at home with my new son. Quitting my job was financially impossible. After all, my husband and I had the perfect plan: we would buy a new home and have a baby; after a few months I would go back to work, hire a babysitter, and progress smoothly in my career without a hitch.

Once I held my son, however, I knew I had to be home with him full time. Finding a way to do that became my challenge.

I took the plunge and resigned from my job. Our household income was cut in half, so to keep my new job as a stay-at-home mom, I needed to find ways to reduce our spending in all areas. It didn't take long to realize that the area with the greatest savings potential was at the grocery store. I didn't know it at the time, but food—groceries—is the second or third largest household spending category for most families. I did not go back to the corporate world. Ten years later I am still a stay-at-home wife and mother.

Having come from a career in consumer sales and marketing I found that "unraveling" the marketing and merchandising techniques used by grocery stores and manufacturers was a lot of fun—like solving a puzzle. And my method worked! In fact, it worked so well that I decided to start a website where I could help others start saving money on groceries too. Over the past five years this project has been far more interesting and rewarding than any corporate job I ever held, and it still allowed me to be home with my sons (yes, we had a second child).

Now I want to teach you how to become a "strategic shopper" like me, using the system I created. You will use your store's weekly sales ads, the coupons in your Sunday newspaper, and my website *CouponMom.com*, where I do all the hard work for you and millions of other shoppers across the U.S. every week.

My strategy is based on simple principles that work in every area of the country, not only in the big cities. And don't worry—you won't have to compromise your quality standards to save money on groceries.

Here's the key: *saving money on groceries is not about changing the way you eat, it's about changing the way you buy the foods you like.* You will learn new, easy shopping strategies, but you won't sacrifice healthy choices for the sake of saving money.

This is not another grocery savings book recommending a complicated coupon organization system that takes hours each month to maintain. And it is not necessary for you to go to several stores each week to find the best grocery prices. The typical shopper is much too busy to invest that kind of time in grocery shopping. Instead, *Greatest Secrets of the*

Coupon Mom is for busy people like you and me who want to save money but need to do it efficiently.

The key to saving money on groceries is to understand the three basic principles of strategic shopping:

1. **Know your grocery prices**

2. **Know your store's savings programs**

3. **Know your grocery coupons**

Once you understand how these three principles work and how to combine them to save even more, you will cut your grocery spending dramatically no matter where you buy groceries.

Plus, you'll get a bonus. I'll also show you how to become a strategic giver! In my quest to save my family money, I discovered needs in my own community. I didn't realize it, but the cupboards of my local food pantry were bare. I decided then and there that on my next shopping trip I would use my coupon strategies to add a few extra bargains to my cart. Delivering those items to the food pantry changed my life.

I began teaching my friends and family how to purchase food for charity by combining grocery coupons and low prices. The remarkable success of these efforts led me to create Cut Out Hunger, and my website makes it easy for people to save dramatically not only on their own groceries, but also for items to donate to charity—all for just pennies.

I am reminded of the saying that if you give a man a fish, he'll eat for a day, but if you teach a man to fish, he'll eat for the rest of his life. And in our case, at a very low price.

I don't have a fish to give you, but if you're ready to learn how to buy high-quality food at a low cost for the rest of your life, get in the boat!

Chapter 1

So You Want to Be a Coupon Expert

My mantra: *saving money on groceries is not about changing the way we eat but changing the way we buy the food we like.* That's what I do, and that's what you can do too.

I wasn't born with the secrets I'm going teach to you. Nor was I born with the grocery-shopping gene. Much of what I now know about grocery shopping is common sense, but a lot I've learned by trial and error.

Over the years I've heard from shoppers who've told me they tried to use grocery coupons in the past but gave up because it was too frustrating and difficult to organize. However, once they started using my approach, they began to save a lot of money and time and were thrilled to share their success with others.

It's possible for you to experience the same success, once you understand the fundamental principles behind what I call "strategic shopping." Believe it or not, it's possible for two families to purchase identical grocery items over the course of a year, and for one of the families to pay twice as much as the other. The family paying more money is not buying different food; they are buying their food differently.

So how does one family pay 50 percent less on its groceries? By understanding three basic principles:

Know your grocery prices

To cut grocery spending, you need to know the prices of the items you buy, the prices of acceptable alternative brands or items, and which of your items have the biggest impact on your grocery bill (meat or cereal, for example). I will teach you exactly how to pay the lowest price possible on your favorite items.

Know your store's savings programs

Every grocery store has a long list of promotional programs, marketing strategies, and membership benefits that shoppers can use to save money. I have counted as many as fifteen savings programs at one grocery store. Many such programs can be combined to realize even more savings.

You need to learn your store's savings programs and how to use them to cut your grocery bill. Don't panic if you don't know this yet. I'll share all my secrets for how to uncover the savings programs at your store.

Know your grocery coupons

With over $318 billion of potential coupon savings available to shoppers each year, you need to know where to find the coupons for the items you like, when to use them, and how to maximize their value[1].

By combining coupons with low prices and savings programs, you can even get many grocery items free over the course of a year. You'll learn how to get your fair share of these potential savings to help cut your grocery bill dramatically.

Learning and practicing these three principles will change your life—really. Together with experience, savings secrets, and my website, you'll save dramatically on groceries in no time!

When I first began tackling our family's grocery spending, I asked my Aunt Jane how she saved on groceries when she was a young mother. I had heard through the family grapevine that she'd managed to feed her small family on $20 a week, which was all they had to spend. She told me she reviewed each of the supermarket flyers, planned meals around what was on sale, and if necessary, used most of a week's budget to stock up, at rock-bottom prices, on main items (such as ground beef or chicken) and freeze them for future weeks. She didn't have the option of shopping only at the one store she preferred; she had to shop at a few stores to make ends meet. She needed to pay the absolute lowest price for each item she purchased.

When I first quit working to be home with my kids and had extra time to shop, I took her advice and began saving dramatically on my groceries overnight.

I refer to my Aunt Jane and these kinds of shoppers as "strategic shoppers." They may go to several stores to buy the best deals each week out of financial necessity, or they may view their grocery shopping expertise as a fun hobby and simply enjoy the thrill of finding and stocking up on bargains. Industry research reports that these kinds of shoppers (who typically use coupons heavily) spend an average of 140 minutes a week in grocery stores finding sale items and searching their coupon collections for matching coupons[2].

No doubt, these shoppers save a lot of money on their groceries, but the reality is that very few shoppers are regular strategic shoppers, which is probably not surprising given the time required.

So how can you benefit without store hopping? You're in luck, because I've done the research for you and I'm here to share it all. My goal is to make it easy for you to save. You don't have to be confused about all your options; you don't have to spend more time trying to save more money.

Habits of Strategic Shoppers

Plan Before You Shop

According to the Food Marketing Institute, the average shopper visits the grocery store twice a week. Most likely, not all of these trips are carefully planned and thus include impulse purchases that drive up the cost of a family's grocery bill.

Having a shopping plan enables a shopper to get in and out of the store quickly, which saves money by reducing impulse purchases. Armed with a plan, shoppers can actually spend less time in the store than those who "shop as they go." Bottom line: you'll spend less time overall on grocery shopping, including the planning time, because you will cut your shopping down to one well-planned trip a week, or even two shorter well-planned trips.

Use the store's weekly sale ad to plan your shopping list. It is important to be familiar with how to get the best deals at more than one of your local grocery stores. You must know how to read the grocery ads to determine if a "sale" item is really a good price or not. You must be able to spot good values and select the store with the lowest prices for the items on your list.

Be Flexible with Store Brands and Store Choices

Since the focus is on getting the best quality and value for your grocery dollars, you need to be open to shopping at more than one store, depending on the best sale prices that week. You must also be willing to try comparable brands of products based on which brand of an item is at a lower price each week.

Plan Your Meals Around Store Specials

The shopping list of someone saving big money at the grocery store each week is no different than anyone else's. The secret is to buy the items on sale. Then plan your menu around those items.

Stick to Your Grocery List and Resist Impulse Purchases

One of the most expensive habits is impulse buying. Studies show a direct correlation between the number of minutes spent in the store and the amount of money spent. Without even using coupons or shopping sales, shoppers can save dramatically by resolving to: (1) make a list before every shopping trip to help them shop efficiently, and (2) vow not to purchase anything else.

Don't Give in to Your Kids' Demands

Every parent knows that taking a child to the grocery store can be a challenge—and expensive. Supermarkets are filled with all kinds of interesting toys, food, and candy that just beg the question, "Mom, can we get this?" Spending only an extra $5 a week on a child's unplanned request adds up to $260 a year, so it pays to find a way to nip this habit in the bud at a young age.

If it's not possible or convenient to leave your kids at home, find ways to make the trip tolerable for everyone. With younger children, reward good behavior (not asking for anything that isn't on the list) by letting them get a free cookie at the bakery at the end of the shopping trip, or giving them a small prize or lollipop that you've brought from home when you get to the checkout line. This worked with my sons when they were young, as long as I had carefully planned my list so I could move quickly and efficiently through the store. You can also involve them by letting them pick out their favorite flavor or variety of certain items on your list.

> *"I am a stay-at-home mom and we really love the savings. My 9-year old daughter went with me the first time I started using your coupon method. She had so much fun. I was showing her the regular price, the sale price and then the coupons! We saved over 56 percent on our bill. What a learning experience for both of us."*
>
> ~ *Sandy, California*

Go to the Store Once a Week

One of the easiest ways to overspend on groceries is by making frequent, short, unplanned trips to the store. Plan one or two comprehensive shopping trips per week, if it's convenient. That's it. This will save you major time and money overall. Fewer trips to the store also lower the risk of impulse shopping.

Know How to Use Grocery Coupons

You knew it was coming! You must understand the timing of grocery coupons—the best time to use a coupon is when the item goes on sale, not necessarily when the coupon first comes out. And never purchase an item just because you have a coupon. Don't be talked into buying something you don't use just because you have a coupon, unless of course an item is free with a coupon. In that case, get the item and donate it to charity.

Try Store Brands

Many store-brand items are actually produced by the same companies that produce their brand-name counterparts. Therefore product quality is comparable at a lower price. This is not true all the time, however, and store brands may not meet your quality expectations. But it's important to your food budget to begin finding store brands you like.

Strategic shoppers know that most major supermarkets offer a guarantee on their store-brand items and will offer a refund if their product quality doesn't meet your expectation. Some stores' guarantees offer the national brand free if you do not find their store-brand item acceptable.

Know Your Prices

You must learn the prices for common grocery items you purchase regularly. As a result you'll easily recognize when an item is a good value. Do not let the size of a grocery display or a "sale" sign sway your purchase decision. Because you are familiar with the high and low prices of your common items, you know when to stock up on favorite items so you never have to pay full price.

Know Your Store's Marketing and Promotional Programs

Pay attention to your store's promotional programs and consider them to be "savings programs" you can use to your advantage. Keep up with a store's savings program through its website, weekly ads, customer-service desk, and store personnel, or even by asking other shoppers.

Once in the habit of using sales, promotional programs, and coupons, strategic shoppers then pay the lowest price for their grocery items—every week.

How to Get Started

The first step is to determine how much you'd like to save on your groceries. Write it down before you begin working on reducing your spending. If you currently spend $150 a week on groceries, learning how to save just $15 a week will add up to $780 a year, which is real money in anyone's book. Cutting your spending in half, which isn't unrealistic, would save you $3,900 per year.

Any degree of savings, as compared to what you have been spending, is success. Determining a realistic goal before you get started will make the process more satisfying, and any changes you make will more likely stick. Your goal may not involve getting the lowest possible price on every item you buy; it can simply be learning how to pay lower prices on some of your items. This still will add up to significant savings over the course of a year.

I receive many letters and emails, so I've learned that grocery-saving success is relative to each shopper's previous habits. I always get a kick out of the difference in perspective. For example, one shopper recently sent me an email thanking me for helping her save 7 percent on her grocery bill. Just a week earlier, another shopper had complained that she was not able to get her savings percentage any higher than 70 percent!

When I decided to start an exercise program, I didn't expect to be a long-distance runner right away. If I had, I'd have given up quickly. My point? Start with a small goal, pat yourself on the back when you reach it, and then decide if you'd like to increase your goal as you become comfortable with new grocery-saving strategies.

The key is having a system that works for you and is realistic given your time constraints. You'll want to stick with it for the long term when you see your savings really add up over time. The shopper who saves 7 percent every single year over her lifetime will save more money than the one who begins by saving 70 percent but gives up after a few months because it takes too much time.

Know Your Prices and Have a Plan

The most common question I get is "Which store offers the lowest prices?" This is not an easy question to answer. Do you mean the lowest regular prices, or the lowest sale prices, or the lowest everyday low prices? No one store offers the lowest prices on all items all the time. The answer is, most stores offer the lowest prices some of the time.

Not what you wanted to hear, I know. It would be easier if one store had the lowest prices on every item every day. Thanks to our free-market economy and healthy competition, however, stores pay close attention to each other's prices and work to attract shoppers by promoting featured prices and savings programs.

It is also difficult to find the best overall prices because every household buys a slightly different selection of grocery items. Considering that the average supermarket today carries twenty-five thousand items, and the typical family may buy fifty to a hundred items a week, we can logically assume that everyone buys different groceries!

I frequently see grocery advertisements featuring comparison pricing on a "typical basket of items," comparing their store to a competitor. Of course, the advertised store always has a lower total price than its competitor. Most likely, the same comparison could be done the following week with reversed results, because the food items listed would be on sale at the competitor's store the following week, and back to regular price at the advertised store. We cannot assume there is one "magic store" where we can expect to pay the lowest price on all of our items all the time.

Identify Your Key Items

The best way to recognize the lowest prices for your grocery needs is to track and observe price fluctuations for your particular key items over a period of time. This is also known as the "price book concept."

A price book shows a record of weekly prices for your key items at your area grocery stores over a period of two to three months. By tracking prices for your items, you learn their highest and lowest prices and which store has the most favorable prices for your key items.

You can do a thorough study of two hundred grocery items at several stores, or you can do what I do—make a mental note of the prices of twenty of your most common grocery items at the stores you visit most often. I call these "high-impact" items, since we buy them frequently and spend the majority of our grocery budget on them.

Create a Price Book

1. Identify your high-impact items. Just open your refrigerator and cupboards to jog your memory, and then make a list of items you use regularly. If you keep grocery receipts, use them to note items and prices paid for each. Track a realistic number of items so the exercise isn't too tedious in the beginning. Once you've come up with your list (twenty is a reasonable number to start) you can always add additional items.

2. Record your information. Make a list of the items and prices you

plan to track. Make columns for each week for the next several weeks. Use a computer spreadsheet or buy a spiral notebook—create a simple system that will work for you.

3. Note the prices of your items when you shop by checking the weekly ad at your store or other stores in the area.

4. Determine the "impact" of each item by multiplying the quantity of each item purchased by its price. The total amount of money spent per week or month on each item will help you zero in on the items with the greatest savings opportunities.

For example, I have found that one of our household's highest impact items is fresh boneless chicken breasts. The lowest price for this item is typically $1.99 per pound, but it can sell for as high as $4.99 per pound in our supermarket. By always purchasing it at $1.99 and freezing extra for future weeks, I save as much as $450 per year on this high-impact item by knowing its lowest price.

Always Make a Shopping List

Strategic shoppers never enter the grocery store without a shopping list. Planning ahead will keep you from succumbing to impulse purchases, and will cut your shopping down to one or two well-planned, efficient trips a week.

One of the most expensive habits shoppers have is impulse buying. That comes as no surprise, because retailers are experts at merchandising, which means they know how to get us to buy. Next time you go shopping, look around at all of the signs that advertise products—signs in your shopping cart, painted on the floor, hanging from the ceiling, displayed at the end of every aisle, even on special tables and displays set up in every available square inch of space.

A couple of years ago I took one of our local television station's consumer reporters on a grocery shopping trip for their news show. He had a great sense of humor and thought my strategic shopping deals were hilarious. At one point, he looked at me and asked, "So if you see an item in the store and it's not on your list, would you get it?" I said yes, of course, if I saw a great unadvertised sale item, I would buy it. He said, "No, I mean if you saw something really neat and it wasn't on sale, you just wanted it, would you get it?"

That one stumped me. I had to think about it. After a couple seconds, I shook my head and said, "No, I never do that." He laughed out loud! Believe me, I did plenty of that when my grocery bill was out of control years ago. But I don't think that way anymore. It is my habit to make a grocery list and stick to it. You can do it too, once you've done it a few times. It will be the smartest and most lucrative habit you ever start.

> "Using the Coupon Mom Best-Deals List is so easy and helpful. Not only does it save me time and money by combining the coupons with the sale items to get the 'ultimate deal', but it actually helps me not to impulse shop. I want to see how much I've saved so if I stick to my shopping list, my chances of saving more are better than if I just start picking things off the shelves, not knowing if there is a coupon out there for those items or not."
>
> ~ Christine, Colorado

Value Shopping

Strategic shopping is not just about getting lower prices; it is about getting the best value for your grocery dollar. You do not have to sacrifice food quality to save money on groceries. Remember my mantra: *saving money on groceries is not about changing the way you eat but changing the way you buy food you like.* In fact, it is far more important to buy healthy food as an investment in your family's well-being than it is to eat unhealthy food because it is low-priced. The trick is figuring out how to buy the healthy groceries you prefer at prices you can afford.

It's possible to have it all—healthy food options, high-quality food sources, and low prices. It is simply a matter of learning the strategic shopping skills so you can eat well at a fraction of the full cost of groceries.

My advice may contradict the traditional grocery-saving advice to "only shop the perimeter of the store" to save money. Items found in the perimeter of the store—such as fresh produce, dairy, and meat products—are less expensive because they are more basic and do not have as much packaging or preparation as the convenience foods and packaged grocery items found in the center of the store. Typically, packaged grocery items do cost more at their regular prices, and the aisles filled with higher-priced grocery items can be an overspending trap for the average shopper. However, by following my " Best-Deals List" (which we'll learn about in chapter. 4), you can confidently take advantage of grocery deals without paying a premium for convenience or packaging.

Additionally, most of us have been told that cooking and baking "from scratch" is less expensive than buying mixes or prepared sauces, dressings, and baked goods. Now, however, you'll be able to buy convenience products at bargain prices, which can be lower than the cost of "from scratch" ingredients. The important thing is to keep an open mind as you take this new approach to saving money on groceries.

Brand Flexibility and Stocking Up

When you first sit down to list the common grocery items you purchase on a regular basis, you may discover that you buy the same items and brands every week. Some shoppers buy specific brands for good reasons, and some simply buy them out of habit. Being willing to be brand flexible rather than brand loyal can save big bucks over the course of a year.

Brand Loyalty

Grocery preferences are personal. Many of us are fiercely loyal to particular brands and will buy them regardless of their price. I agree that in some cases there are superior brands. However, our brand perceptions are also strongly affected by good product marketing. If you have ever worked in a marketing job, you know how difficult it can be to convince consumers that your product is better than a competitor's perfectly good product. Expensive advertising helps establish brand preferences, but that advertising cost is invariably passed along to the consumer as a price premium, which shoppers are willing to pay because the advertising was effective!

Fortunately many of the companies that advertise the most also promote their products heavily with sale prices and coupons. By timing your purchases to coincide with sales and coupons, and then stocking up on items at their rock-bottom prices, you may be able to enjoy your favorite name-brand items at bargain prices.

Brand Flexibility

As you identify and list your common grocery items, identify those items that you may be willing to consider as "brand flexible." You may always buy the same brand of dishwashing liquid, toothpaste, or laundry detergent regardless of price. Our brand preferences may be based on what our parents bought when we were growing up, or we might simply buy out of habit. By trying the competitor's brand (especially at a rock-bottom deal) you may find their product is perfectly adequate. Trying store brands can also save money, and many store chains offer a satisfaction guarantee for their own store brands, so it is no risk to try them. Being brand flexible on even a few items can yield significant savings in a year's time.

For example, when I first did this exercise with my family's grocery items, I found we purchased the same brand of juice drink every week, regardless of price. When I looked at the annual cost of this fairly insignificant item, I was shocked! The juice drink cost an average of $7.50 a week, or $390 per year. We tried some reasonable substitutes, and after a few tries discovered that bottled lemonade was just as good, and cost an average of $2.50 a week. This small change saved us $260 per year!

Stocking Up

Once you have identified your key items and their price ranges, it won't be long until you can easily see what is available at rock-bottom prices. By stocking up on your key items at the lowest prices, you will never have to pay full price again, and will dramatically cut your grocery spending.

In deciding on the quantity you need to keep on hand of your key items, consider the following factors:

1. Determine the quantity of your key items that you use in a six-week to three-month time period. Buy that supply when they are at a rock-bottom price. Most likely another coupon will come out for these items within three months, and the item's sale cycle (varying from highest to lowest price) is typically two to three months, so you can expect to stock up every few months. If you are brand flexible, you'll be able to stock up on various brands in a shorter period of time, so you will not need to keep as many items on hand.

Recently I read a question written by a shopper who had more than one hundred boxes of dry pasta (purchased at no cost with coupons). She wanted to know how long that pasta would be okay to eat. If her family ate as many as two boxes of pasta a week, this shopper would have a full year's supply of pasta on hand—at least four times the amount her family needed.

Strategic shoppers learn to use the stocking-up strategy within reason, and then work to stock the shelves of area food pantries with items purchased from extra coupons. Obviously, having a more reasonable supply of extra food items is easier to manage and presents fewer food-safety concerns.

2. It is important to know how long food items last and to rotate your stored food supply. Most products have a date or a code printed on the package that indicates freshness. These dates do not necessarily mean that the product has to be discarded after the date. There are different definitions for these dates:

Sell-by date: Tells the store how long to display the product for sale. You should buy the product before the date expires.

Best if used by (or before) date: Recommended for best flavor or quality. It is not a purchase or safety date.

Use-by date: The last date recommended for the use of product while at peak quality. The date has been determined by the manufacturer of the product.

Closed or coded dates: Packing numbers for use by the manufacturer in tracking their products. This enables manufacturers to rotate their stock as well as locate their products in the event of a recall.

Expired dates: As long as a product is wholesome, a retailer may legally sell fresh or processed meat and poultry products beyond the expiration date on the package[3].

Most canned foods have a long "health life," and when properly stored, are safe to eat for several years:

- *Baby food:* Do not buy or use infant formula and baby food past its "use-by" date. Federal regulations require a date on those products.

- *Low-acid canned goods:* Two to five years [canned meat and poultry, stews, soups (except tomato), pasta products, potatoes, corn, carrots, spinach, beans, beets, peas, and pumpkin].

- *High-acid canned goods:* Twelve to eighteen months (tomato products, fruits, sauerkraut, and foods in vinegar-based sauces or dressings)[4].

Tools for Effective Shopping

Once you've established the lowest prices on your high-impact items and have learned a little about pricing strategies, you're off to a good start on grocery savings. The next step is to add the coupons. You do not need to spend a fortune on fancy coupon organizational systems to be a successful strategic shopper. If you keep it simple you will be more likely to stick with this new way of shopping and saving. I recommend that your "starter kit" include:

- A spiral notebook to record prices and keep weekly shopping lists (or a computer spreadsheet if you prefer)

- A plastic check organizer to store cut-out coupons, typically found at an office supply store or in the office supply aisle of the grocery store for $3 or less

- An annual subscription to your city's largest newspaper to get home delivery of Sunday coupons. If you do not have one now, you should call the newspaper and ask for their "new subscriber" rate or best introductory offer. Also, check with your grocery store to see if they sell discounted Sunday newspapers later in the day on Sunday or on Monday, which may be a less-expensive alternative

- A large pair of scissors to cut coupons (it goes much faster than using small scissors)

- My website address: *CouponMom.com*

"Thank you for this GREAT site! I have been trying to do this on my own for years and it takes HOURS a week just to get what I thought was the lowest grocery prices. Now, I can save time and effort and still get more for less because you list the unadvertised sale prices too. In just two weeks, the stress from every day life has decreased just because I have found several more hours per week that I can now devote to my family. Of course, the money I save has increased too. And it's my pleasure to share some of what I reap with those who can't afford it. It's worth it - many times over."

~ Deliana, California

If you do not have a computer or a printer, you do not need one. Internet access is free at public libraries, and my site is free to use. Simply access the site and write down the deals information you need each week.

Chapter 2

Top Ten Coupon Myths

Before we go further, we need to talk about something. You don't like using coupons. Maybe you even hate using coupons. Unless you are part of the 15 percent of shoppers who use coupons religiously, you likely have a logical reason for not shopping with coupons.

I've used coupons for over a decade, and for the past five years I've spoken to thousands of people about using coupons to save money and donate food to charity. I have learned what people don't like about coupons, and in some cases, I agree with their objections. Invariably shoppers across the country object to the same challenges and share common misconceptions about coupons.

When checking out at the grocery store, other shoppers frequently look at me incredulously and ask, "You really like coupons, don't you?" I like to reply, "Well actually, I really like my money. Using coupons is one way to have more of it."

In 2004 shoppers saved almost $3 billion with grocery coupons, a substantial sum. However, the number that gets my attention is the $315-billion worth of grocery coupons that were thrown away[1]. In spite

of massive advertising and promotion by the grocery and coupon indus-
tries, fewer than 2 percent of coupons are converted into real money. In
my opinion, coupon redemption is low because clipping and using
coupons is time-consuming for people who are already busy. But we also
know that more than 2 percent of people in our country have real financial needs and could benefit from some of that $315 billion being thrown
away. So what's the solution?

I believe the answer to helping more people save money is to make it
easier for people to use grocery coupons. Organizing coupon information
and identifying good coupon deals for people is the key. My website has
successfully helped thousands of people save millions of dollars since its
inception in March 2001.

Whether your personal goal is to save $10 or $100 a week on your
groceries, you can achieve your grocery-savings objective much easier
than you can imagine. I started *CouponMom.com* in an effort to make it
easier for non-coupon-users to shop for charity with coupons. I even tested it using eight-year-olds. It is not impossible. But first, let's examine the
most common challenges of using coupons and how my program can help
you save real money.

Myth #1

My family doesn't use the products that have grocery coupons. We don't eat processed foods.

It's not true that coupons are only for processed, unhealthy foods. In fact,
many coupons are available for fresh items like cheese, yogurt, cottage
cheese, eggs, milk, and occasionally fresh produce. There are many
coupons for common frozen foods—vegetables, ice cream (is this
processed? Most households eat it!), pizzas, bagels, and many conven-

ience foods. I wouldn't buy dry cereal without a coupon; and peanut butter, condiments, baking mixes, coffee, tea, crackers, cookies, snacks,
pasta sauces, pasta, rice, and fruit juices commonly have coupons.

Coupons also follow food trends, so now companies issue more
coupons for organic foods and products designed for special dietary
needs. Finally, a high percentage of grocery coupons fall into the categories of household cleaning products, paper products, and personal-care
products such as shampoo and toothpaste. In fact, 47 percent of coupons
issued are for nonfood items. There are more coupons issued for household cleaning products than any other type of coupon[2].

Myth #2

It takes too much time to clip
and organize coupons.

I hear you! I also hate cutting out and organizing hundreds of coupons, so
I don't. But I do save thousands of dollars a year on groceries. My system
eliminates 90 percent of the manual labor, frustration, and drudgery of
coupon organization, while still allowing you to save big money. I came up
with a searchable, sortable online database of all the coupons issued in the
Sunday newspaper. Think of it as the Dewey decimal system of grocery
coupons.

To maximize your coupon savings you really need to save all the grocery coupons each week. You never know what will be on sale in the
future, making the item free or practically free with a coupon. However,
there can be up to two hundred coupons a week in the Sunday paper,
which would take hours each month to cut out, organize, and search
through every time you need a coupon. You would also have to spend a

lot of time regularly checking your entire coupon collection for expired coupons.

My website makes it possible to save all of the coupons without having to cut them out until you need them. It even takes care of deleting expired coupon offers from the database automatically. Realistically, even the most diligent coupon user only uses 10 percent of the coupons issued. Voila—just cut out the few coupons you need each week, and you'll save real money with 90 percent less effort.

> *"I stumbled across your site quite by accident. I love that I can organize the list and the coupon lists as I see fit. I already had a great personal system for organizing my coupons, and combining that with your list takes a lot of strain out of my shopping. I love Cut Out Hunger, and I've told everyone about it."*
>
> *~ Carol*

Myth #3

I don't use grocery coupons because it's cheaper to just buy the store brands and use my store discount card.

Although buying store brands and using the store's discount card are important components of strategic shopping, in many cases a name-brand item on sale with a coupon is much less expensive than the store brand. I agree that it may not make sense to buy a name-brand product with a coupon if the store brand is less expensive and of equal quality, but that's not always the case.

Using the store discount card does not take the place of saving even more with coupons. Shoppers can get low sale prices with the store dis-count card and then use a grocery coupon to bring the item's price down even lower; the two strategies are not mutually exclusive. Finally, you may not be aware of the new coupon programs available that help you save money on some store brands! I'll teach you about that easy program too.

When I first appeared on *Good Morning America* in April 2004, their producers wanted to test the theory that store brands are always cheap-er, so they set up a real shopping competition between their reporter, Lara Spencer, and me. We had identical shopping lists in terms of the types of items. Lara's strategy was to buy the lowest-priced items, whether they were name brand or store brand, without using coupons. My strategy was to use my Best-Deals List, buying name-brand items with grocery coupons. Lara's final total was $78, while mine was $35. And this was in one of America's most expensive cities, in a store I had never set foot in before. Lara even asked local shoppers to help her find the best deals and lowest prices for her listed items, and they knew all about their own store!

Myth #4

I don't have the time to go to different grocery stores to save money.

It may be true that going to several grocery stores a week to buy each store's lowest-priced deals will save money overall, but the average shop-per struggles to find the time to get to one grocery store once a week. My strategic-shopping approach focuses on the easiest methods for shop-pers to save the most money in the least amount of time. The objective is to learn how to maximize grocery savings at their preferred store by understanding: (1) price ranges for their own specific grocery items, (2) how the store's savings programs work, and (3) how to combine them with coupons to save money easily and efficiently.

After years of tracking prices at several stores within the same city, I have learned that the same grocery deals generally cycle through every major supermarket in a city. In other words, shoppers do not need to go to every store in one week to get the best deals; they could just shop at one or two preferred stores and wait for the sales to cycle through their own store.

The key is simply knowing how to put the best deals together at your own store by understanding specific savings program strategies. I'll explain exactly what questions to ask regarding your store's savings programs and how to use them. You'll be amazed how much you'll save without going to several stores.

Myth #5

It isn't worth it to use coupons to save 20 or 30 cents.

Any one of us would bend over and pick up a quarter we saw lying on the ground. The reality is, the average coupon is worth far more than 20 cents (93 cents was the average face value of coupons distributed in 2003) and if your supermarket doubles or triples coupons, the value is much higher. The bulk of all coupons distributed have a face value of $1, and 7 percent of coupons have a face value of $2[3].

In fact, the average face value of coupons increased by 9.4 percent from 2003 to 2004, which is higher than the Consumer-Price-Index growth. With one hundred to two hundred coupons distributed in the Sunday paper every week, it is likely that most coupon users would take advantage of several coupons, not just one. Regular coupon users save far more than 20 or 30 cents. Industry research shows that they save an average of 11.5 percent off their total shopping bill.

Myth #6

To be effective with coupons
I have to subscribe to a newspaper.

If you don't get the Sunday newspaper you can still save money with coupons by getting them from other sources (direct mailings, magazine inserts, the Internet, and other ideas I'll share later in the book). However, 82 percent of coupons issued are in the Sunday newspaper, representing $261 billion of the potential coupon savings available to shoppers. That is why my website provides specific online coupon databases of the Sunday newspaper coupons.

If you want to take advantage of these savings, buy the paper and let yourself off the hook if you don't have time to read it. Just tell yourself you are buying the paper for the financial value of the coupons and then use the rest of it to line your cat box, make paper-mache piñatas or to wash your windows.

Most likely you'll appreciate being able to scan the headlines when you do have time, to check the movie schedule easily, and to see your children take an interest in reading the news or even the comics. Remember, the newspaper also carries many valuable coupons for restaurants and stores. Your coupon savings will far outweigh the cost of the newspaper. In fact, smart coupon users buy more than one copy of the Sunday paper!

> *"I was a total skeptic that I could cut my grocery bill. I took the Kroger ad and my coupons that I found within about 10 minutes (using your simplified system), and my husband, kids and I drove to Kroger (about 12 miles away). We bought almost $300 worth of groceries for $150. Plus I have a $10.00 rebate that I will be able to mail in, which brings the total to $140. I couldn't*

believe it. We applied for the Kroger-plus card while we were at the store. The lady behind me couldn't believe how much I saved and how much food, detergent, and soda I bought. My husband and I are going to start getting the Sunday newspaper and clipping coupons religiously."

~ Amanda, Michigan

Myth #7

I don't have time to go through all of the store ads to match sales with coupons.

The Internet has made it easy to share such information as weekly grocery deals. In fact, thousands of shoppers take advantage of subscription websites and shopping services that do the work of reviewing the sale items in store ads and matching them to that city's Sunday newspaper coupons. By eliminating the hour it takes to do this, far busier shoppers are able to save dramatically on their groceries just by using my website.

Myth #8

I cannot afford to donate food to charity.

My website is designed to help shoppers, even the busiest ones, save money easily by finding grocery deals in all categories. If a grocery deal is appropriate for a typical food pantry, the item will include the designation "Charity." When shoppers see these rock-bottom deals (which may even be free with a coupon) and their family doesn't use that item, it's easy to buy the item and save it in a box to donate to a local food pantry.

Many shoppers have reported being able to donate hundreds of dollars of food a year, or even a month, at virtually no cost to their families.

> *"I'm on a fixed income and it's been so wonderful to be able to not only save money for myself but to provide donations to the local Interfaith charity. Without your help, I wouldn't be able to do a fraction of the donating I do now."*
>
> ~ *Wendy, California*

They save dramatically on their own groceries and experience the joy and satisfaction of helping families in their own backyard. *CouponMom.com* can help anyone, regardless of income, practice this kind of generosity.

Myth #9

Only poor people use coupons.

This perception of coupon users couldn't be farther from the truth. In fact, there are more coupon users in higher income brackets than lower income brackets.

Over 80 percent of shoppers with household incomes of $50,000 to $75,000 a year report using coupons to grocery shop. Industry statistics also found that 74 percent of households earning more than $75,000 a year use grocery coupons. The lowest level of coupon use (70 percent) is in the $25,000-to-$50,000 annual income bracket[4].

I do not know the reasons behind these statistics, but they definitely prove that coupon usage is simply a smart way for consumers of all income levels to save money. The reason *CouponMom.com* is free to users is to make it easier for families of all income levels to save money and donate food to charity. Families without computers can take advantage of free Internet access at public libraries to use the savings program.

Myth #10

You can save more at wholesale clubs, and they don't accept coupons.

Shopping in bulk at wholesale clubs can be a good way to save money on many items. However, some items are much less expensive at traditional supermarkets when purchased with a coupon, particularly if the supermarket doubles coupons. This book will help you determine which shopping option makes the most sense for you, based on the grocery items you prefer and your geographic and time constraints.

Are you ready? It's time to start saving!

Chapter 3

So Many Stores, So Little Time

With so many shopping options available, it is easy to be confused about which store offers the best prices and value. Let's begin by defining the most common types of stores and their pricing strategies.

Common Pricing Strategies

The Everyday-Low-Price Store

The strategy at these stores is to price their products at a relatively low price every day, without using weekly sales features and promotional programs. Regular prices are usually lower than a supermarket's regular prices. Everyday-low-price stores (such as Super Wal-Mart) do not feature deeply discounted sale items each week but advertise consistent low prices. Some accept grocery coupons, but probably do not offer double- or triple-coupon promotions. These stores can be a good option for the shopper who does not want to take the time to review store ads or grocery coupons.

The High-Low-Price Store

These stores are generally traditional supermarkets that promote deeply discounted prices on "featured" items in their weekly ad and offer promotional programs to attract shoppers. Prices on their featured items tend to be lower than the everyday low prices at Super Wal-Mart type stores. However, high-low-price stores (such as Albertsons, Kroger, and Safeway) count on shoppers purchasing the higher-priced items in their store to compensate for the low-profit margins on their featured items. Some featured items are actually sold at a loss (called "loss leaders") to attract shoppers. You will save the most by stocking up on featured items at high-low stores and use coupons to pay the lowest prices possible.

Wholesale Clubs and Warehouse Stores

Wholesale clubs (like Costco and Sam's Club) and warehouse stores (such as Food 4 Less and ALDI) tend to have lower regular prices than high-low stores' regular prices, with limited services and selection. As a result, they have lower overhead costs than full-service supermarkets. Their strategy is to attract shoppers with items sold in larger bulk packaging at a lower cost per unit. Most wholesale clubs do not accept coupons, but warehouse stores do, generally.

The Service Store

These stores (Whole Foods is one example) appeal to shoppers who are less motivated by price, focusing on high-quality products and an expanded selection of products to attract shoppers. Some stores even provide in-store entertainment and events to attract service-focused shoppers. These shoppers prefer stores with extra services and an expanded selection of items. Service stores tend to charge higher prices than the other three types of stores. Some service stores do take a high-low pricing approach (such as Harris Teeter and Publix).

With so many shopping options available, pricing is important. But most shoppers live near a supermarket, so store location is a key determinant for the average shopper. And because the average shopper's time is limited, traditional grocery stores and supermarkets see the most traffic. That's why I focus on how to maximize your saving at the store that has the broadest national distribution. In addition, national statistics support the fact that there are far more supermarkets than other types of shopping options, and most of the grocery dollars spent in this country are at supermarkets. So this is where strategic shopping works best.

Wholesale Club Considerations

A common debate among shoppers is whether wholesale clubs (Costco or Sam's Club) are a better bargain than shopping at supermarkets. Each side has equally compelling arguments. My observation is that there is no absolute for all shoppers; each one needs to determine what makes sense given their own situation. To make the best decision, ask yourself a few questions:

1. *How far is the club store from your house?* What will it cost you in gas to get to that store? If your wholesale club store is closer, this may not be a factor for you, but it's important to consider.

2. *What is the annual membership cost of the club store?* Perhaps you own a business that could buy the membership and thus benefit from purchasing privileges at a club store. Perhaps your employer provides a free membership for employees. Check for introductory membership rates available at newly opened locations, or special promotions available on the club's website. Remember to factor the cost of the club membership into the savings equation.

3. *Does your supermarket have store-brand alternatives for your common*

items? Although the unit cost of a name-brand item at a wholesale club may be less expensive than a supermarket name-brand item, most national supermarket chains have comprehensive store-brand lines providing alternatives for most items. If the supermarket store-brand item meets your quality standards, its unit cost may be less expensive than buying the name-brand item in bulk at the club store. Therefore be sure to include store-brand alternatives (for both the club and the supermarket) in your price comparisons.

4. *How large is your household?* For large households, the lower unit cost of the larger packaging of club-store products may make sense because large quantities won't go to waste.

5. *Do you have room to store large quantities?* If so, taking advantage of low prices on meat and chicken to freeze for future weeks may make sense. However, compare these prices closely with your supermarket's rock-bottom sale prices to see if they are lower than the wholesale club's everyday prices on similar cuts of meat or chicken.

6. *How disciplined are you at resisting impulse spending?* The risk of shopping at wholesale clubs or discount merchandisers for groceries is that you will be tempted to buy "great bargains" in the non-grocery departments.

7. *Does your club store accept grocery coupons?* Some do, so it's worth asking. BJ's Wholesale Club, for example, has printable coupons on its website.

Some strategic shoppers shop the best deals with coupons at their supermarket and also go to club stores to stock up on those best bargains. Club shoppers report these best deals at their stores:

Club Food Bargains	Club Non-Food Bargains
Milk	Gas
Spaghetti sauce	Brand name clothing
Microwave popcorn	Film developing
Peanut butter	Baby wipes
Juice boxes	Christmas decorations
Pickles	Laundry detergent
Sugar-free sweeteners	Tires
Instant hot chocolate	Batteries

Source: Good Housekeeping magazine, January 2005

It does not make sense to provide an exhaustive pricing comparison between specific supermarkets and wholesale clubs in this book because grocery prices and store coupon policies vary across the country. Additionally, shoppers' household sizes, cash flow constraints, storage space, and overall situations are very different. Shoppers really need to compare the actual cost, divided into unit costs, of their key items and also consider store-brand substitutes that may be acceptable to your household.

My response to "which store has the lowest prices" is that you can save money by learning how to be a strategic shopper at any store, as long as you know the price points (high and low) of your commonly purchased items. You just need to know how the savings programs work at your stores and know how to use the many types of grocery coupons and promotions available. The store you prefer can be the lowest-priced store if you know how to shop strategically.

Save by Shopping at More Than One Store

In preparing my price comparisons, I was surprised at the wide range of pricing between basic grocery items I purchase at two supermarkets in my area.

Without even looking for sales and using coupons, you can begin saving dramatically by educating yourself on the regular prices of your common grocery items. Let me demonstrate this for you with these simple examples.

I purchase flour on a regular basis. One store's five-pound bag of flour is regularly priced at 99 cents, and the other store's five-pound bag of flour is $1.69 (the name-brand flour is $1.89 at both stores). The same variance holds true for several other of my family's favorite items. Although the 70-cent difference in the flour example may seem small, when multiplied by several items purchased several times over the course of a year, that can add up to hundreds of dollars.

Each store "won" at having the lowest price on half of the items as you will see on page 40, so based on my family's grocery needs, it makes sense to shop at two stores on a regular basis. Fortunately the two stores are within half a mile of each other, so I do not have additional driving time or gasoline expenses to consider. I simply plan two shorter shopping lists each week based on best prices at each store, and plan them several days apart (about the same time we need more bananas and milk). Again, the time savings and dollar savings justify the additional effort of planning two lists.

You may be surprised to learn where your grocery dollar goes. I would expect that main-meal ingredients (meat, chicken, and other dinner entrees) would be a significant percentage of grocery spending, but industry statistics show that only 8 percent of the grocery dollar is spent on main meal ingredients. An astounding 11 percent of our grocery dollar is spent on beverages, and another 6 percent is spent on snack foods[1]. The good news is that snack and beverage items are highly "couponable."

Once you've determined the price ranges for your common items, you can easily spot one at its lowest price. If it seems overwhelming to compare prices for all of them, then narrow the list down to fewer items where you spend the bulk of your grocery dollars (such as meat, produce, dairy products, and dry grocery items you purchase weekly).

It is not unusual for a grocery item's price to fluctuate widely over a few months (for example, a box of cereal at its regular price may be $4.29, but it can go as low as $1.50 on sale). Even without using coupons you will save dramatically if you can recognize your key items' rock-bottom sale prices so you can stock up and never have to pay full price.

You can also begin cutting your grocery bill dramatically by reducing the price you pay for your highest-impact items. For example, buying the five-pound bag of flour at the lower price of 99 cents will save you 70 cents. If you use one bag per month, you save 71 cents per month by knowing the best price for the flour. However, if you routinely purchase three pounds of boneless chicken breasts each week, regardless of the price, and we assume it is on sale at your store one week per month, you pay an average of $3.67 per pound, or $48 per month. In this shopper's case, the flour is not a high-impact item but the chicken is.

The following chart illustrates how strategic shopping can have a significant financial impact over the course of a year. For the sake of simplicity, we will assume the regular price remains constant all year, even though the items will go on sale and their prices do fluctuate throughout the year (equally at each store, most likely, so the relative comparison assumed here is accurate).

Items purchased weekly	Regular Price Store A	Regular Price Store B	Annual Amount Store A	Annual Amount Store B
Romaine Lettuce per head (2)	$1.99	**$1.29**	$207	**$134**
English muffins (2)	**$1.09**	$1.49	**$114**	$155
Saltines (1)	$1.49	**$.97**	$77	**$50**
Ice Cream half gallon (2)	**$2.00**	$2.80	**$208**	$291
Ground Beef (3 pounds)	**$1.50 per lb.**	$1.89 per lb.	**$234**	$295
Total spent on these items per year			$840 per year Store A Shopper	$925 per year Store B Shopper

Shopper C purchases the **BEST DEALS** at each store: **$740** per year
12 percent less than Store A Shopper
20 percent less than Store B Shopper

Although the specific prices listed here are hypothetical, they accurately illustrate how prices can vary by store on many basic items. Using these prices, you can see why small price differences can add up over time. Although the shopper who did all her spending at store A spent less than the store B shopper, shopper C took advantage of each store's best deals and saved the most, between 12 percent and 20 percent less than the "one-store" shoppers. This example illustrates that if I were a shopper who only shopped at one store, I would spend significantly more in a year than the shopper who strategically purchased his or her items at two stores.

Alternative Shopping Options

If you are willing to shop at different types of stores, you can save more on your common grocery items at different sources. Stocking up during monthly (or semimonthly) trips to alternative stores (such as food outlets, health-food stores with bulk aisles, drugstores, or discount stores) can save you big money. When I first began tackling our family's grocery bill, I learned that some items we used regularly were not good buys at the grocery store. I began searching for better buys on these items (which were generally not perishable) so I could stock up monthly and save.

For example, personal-care products, cleaning products, and paper products are fairly expensive at traditional supermarkets at their regular prices. It is possible to buy these items at extremely low prices when they are on sale with a doubled coupon at the supermarket, but their regular prices are generally higher than at a discount merchandiser (like Wal-Mart or Target) or in larger quantities at a club store. Because my supermarket doubles coupons and I have multiple sets of coupons, I purchase these items at our supermarket, but only at their lowest price points. By using this strategy, I frequently get personal-care items (like toothpaste and deodorant) free or for pennies, and am able to stock up with extra coupons.

However, if your supermarket does not double coupons or if your newspaper does not have many coupons, it may make more sense to seek out the lowest-priced drugstore or discount merchandiser for personal-care and household products.

Non-traditional stores (outlets, dollar stores, health-food stores, and discounters) also can be good sources of some select grocery bargains. For example, many cities have bakery outlets that sell bread and baked goods at half price (or less). We have had very good luck buying name-brand English muffins, bagels, cereal bars, pizza crusts, all kinds of breads, coffeecakes, donuts, and more at a bakery outlet store near us. We pay 75 percent less than the regular prices at the supermarket and freeze enough to last a few weeks.

A good source for pantry staples such as gourmet spices, flour, grains, rice, beans, legumes, and nuts is the bulk-food aisle of a local health-food store or natural market. If you like to bake bread, bagels, pretzels, or pizza crusts, it is much less expensive (as much as 80 percent less) to buy yeast by the ounce than to pay for individual packets. Simply keep it in the refrigerator and it will last for a couple of months.

It is also much less expensive to buy very small amounts of gourmet spices (for less than 25 cents) than to pay more than $4 for a whole jar at the grocery store. You also get fresher spices for better flavor, rather than storing the same jar of cumin in your cupboard for ten years. Basic spices (cinnamon, pepper, basil, oregano, and chili powder) are far less expensive at discount stores and drugstores (as low as 50 cents a jar) than at the supermarket.

"Dollar" stores are a recent addition to the grocery market and can be a great source for bargains. You may have to go through some trial and error to see which products meet your quality standards, but that can be worth the potential savings if you find some winners. The increased growth of these chains has brought them to cities all over the country, so they are convenient to many shoppers.

Considering store options outside of your favorite supermarket may provide enlightening information to save your household hundreds of dollars on groceries every year. As you learn to locate the bargains for your common grocery items and then plan your shopping accordingly, your shopping will become more efficient and less expensive.

Whether you alternate shopping locations or take shorter trips to several stores, you will find that strategic shopping pays big dividends.

Chapter 4

Cut the Cost of Groceries with the Best-Deals List

When my family needed to reduce our spending dramatically, I tracked and categorized our spending to see where our money was going. I began to view any savings I could find as my "earnings," my financial contribution to our family. Thinking of budgeting in that light made it more interesting and intellectually challenging for me. It wasn't deprivation. Remember: any money saved is equivalent to after-tax earnings, so it's money in your pocket. Therefore if I could save $400 per month on groceries alone, that would be the equivalent of earning $7,200 per year in a part-time job—and with far less effort!

Outside of the fixed expenses we couldn't change easily (like our mortgage and taxes), our grocery spending was the highest variable, or "fixable," expense. National statistics supported what I found in our own budget: food spending is the third-highest expense in the typical American family's budget. In fact, the average family of four with two children in the United States spends between $503 to $977 per month on groceries[1]. Families who cut their grocery spending by only 20 percent would save

$1,207 to $2,345 per year in after-tax dollars. Therefore making an effort to reduce food spending has the highest potential impact on most household budgets.

I quickly became a "strategic shopper" and compared several stores' prices for our most frequently used items. I shopped at more than one store a week to take advantage of weekly deals, cooked many items from scratch, used grocery coupons, bought store brands, and purchased some items in bulk from the health-food store. I was able to cut our grocery bill from $600 per month to $200-$300 per month in an expensive city. I was amazed at how much we were saving.

To the average grocery shopper, that amount of effort is unrealistic. Most Americans want to save money, but they do not have the time I did to invest in organizing coupons, analyzing store sales flyers, and shopping at multiple stores each week.

The solution? Make it easier for people to save money on their groceries by using the Internet. In September 2000 I began to teach friends and neighbors how to buy food for charity with my strategic-shopping skills. I knew I could easily teach them how to analyze the store ads, organize coupons, and determine the best deals each week.

The marketing person in me immediately recognized an opportunity. What if I provided a weekly list of grocery deals, made it available on a website that anyone could access, and helped shoppers save money? They could take advantage of my free research, and I could suggest they donate some items to charity in exchange for the service.

It took very little time to publish my own list of deals on my website. The savings and charitable benefit of the information multiplied exponentially! I had already seen the concept "convert" average shoppers to my strategic-shopping approach. Best of all, the potential number of site users was unlimited with the same amount of effort on my part.

Because the prices on my stores' Best-Deals Lists were effective across the entire state of Georgia, it was possible to raise awareness of the program through the media. The number of users grew to over a thousand in the first year. The first survey of my website users in January 2002 found that over 20 percent of site users donated food to charity on a regular basis as a result of using the website. The concept was working!

I continue to provide comprehensive Best-Deals Lists every week, available to shoppers seven days a week. I believe shoppers are far more likely to use the site consistently if it is useful for their own family. Therefore I provide a full-service grocery deals website, rather than limiting the list of deals to a handful of best charity deals that perhaps is used annually for food-drive purchases. Shoppers are more likely to donate food on a weekly basis if there's a financial benefit to use the site for their own families. Obviously the impact of weekly, rather than just annual, food donations on local food pantries could be dramatic as the number of shoppers grows.

> *"Your Best-Deals List has literally saved my family of four thousands and thousands of dollars in the past few years. I always check your website first for any deals before going grocery shopping. Even though I clipped coupons before finding your website, you have increased my savings by at least 50%. Not only are you saving us money, but you are helping us to provide food to the needy in our community for pennies!"*
>
> *~ Kendra*

The Best-Deals Lists

Each week the best advertised sale items at several grocery chains in every region of the country are featured on my Best-Deals Lists. We do all the work.

The research of spotting sale items and matching them with appropriate coupons from the newspaper or from Internet coupon sites is all done for you. To do this on your own would take an expert coupon shopper at least thirty minutes a week, and far longer for the less experienced. The savings that coupon shoppers realize would definitely justify the time spent, but most shoppers just don't have the time. So checking the Best-Deals List each week saves you all that research time, and that means saving money. Using the Best-Deals List is simple.

1. Go to *CouponMom.com* (Note: both *CutOutHunger.org* and *CouponMom.com* are my Internet addresses and will take you to the same site so it does not matter which address you use.)

2. Find your state and store. If your store is not listed, use the Virtual Coupon Organizer, which I will explain in chapter 7.

3. When you get to the page with your store's list, you will see a table with eight columns like the one on the following page:

#1	#2	#3	#4	#5	#6	#7	#8
Date Cpn Issued	Advertised Sale Items 11/28 to 12/4	Sale Price	Qty	Cpn. Face $	Total Cpn $	Final Price	% Saved
Print SS	Hormel chili with beans, **CHARITY!**	$0.75	1	$0.50	$0.75	FREE	100%
11/7V	Libby's canned vegetables; **CHARITY!**	$0.33	3	$0.50	$1.00	FREE	100%
10/10S	Bic Twin Select shavers 10-pack; **CHARITY!**	$1.64	1	$1.25	$1.25	$0.39	88%
11/7S2	Hormel chili with beans; **CHARITY!**	$0.75	2	$1.00	$1.00	$0.25	87%
Print Cpn	Advil Liquigels 290 ct. print FREE coupon HERE	$2.64	1	$2.00	$2.00	$0.64	82%
11/7V	Finesse shampoo Buy One Get One FREE (Assumes 2 cpns); **CHARITY!**	$1.65	2	$1.00	$2.00	$0.65	80%
11/7V	Thermasilk shampoo Buy One Get One Free (Use 2 cpns); **CHARITY!**	$1.65	2	$1.00	$2.00	$0.65	80%
11/14V	Del Monte canned pineapple 20 oz.; **CHARITY!**	$0.64	3	$0.50	$1.00	$0.31	76%
9/26V	Keebler Fudge Shoppe cookies (cpn. Expires 11/30)	$1.49	2	$0.75	$1.50	$0.74	74%
11/7V	Birds Eye baby blends vegetables 14-16 oz. Bag	$1.49	1	$0.35	$0.70	$0.79	74%
10/24V	Del Monte canned tomatoes 14.5 oz.; **CHARITY!**	$0.64	3	$0.40	$0.80	$0.37	71%
10/17S	Pillsbury Cake Mix	$0.89	3	$1.00	$1.00	$0.56	71%

Column 1: Coupon source (if it is an Internet coupon) or the date the coupon was published or issued along with the first initial of the circular's name (if the coupon came out in the Sunday paper). For example, the first item shows "Print SS," which is a direct link to the SmartSource.com coupon site where a Hormel chili coupon can be printed. The second item shows that the coupon for Libby's vegetables came out on "11/7V," which indicates November 7 in the Valassis circular.

SmartSource and *Valassis* are both labeled on the top of the front page of the circular each week. Special circulars for specific grocery manufacturers may come out on a monthly, bimonthly, or quarterly basis from Procter & Gamble (noted as PG), Kroger (noted as Kg), Ralphs (noted as Rl), or Kraft (noted as Kf). As new companies introduce their own circulars, the website will explain any new codes.

Column 2: Item description. In addition to describing the item, we also indicate if the item is a good item for food pantries (noted by the word "charity"). On the list shown here, the first two items are actually free with a coupon, and they are both ideal items for charity. This is a perfect example of how easily we can donate to charity at no cost.

Column 3: Sale price of the item.

Column 4: Quantity you would need to buy to take advantage of the coupon or the minimum purchase requirements of the store's price.

Column 5: Face value of the coupon available in the newspaper coupon circular from that particular area.

Column 6: Total coupon savings according to that particular store's coupon policy, depending on whether they double or triple coupons. For example, this store doubles coupons up to 99 cents, so the Keebler cookies' 75-cent coupon is actually worth $1.50 off two packages.

Column 7: Final price of each item after the coupons are deducted from the sale price. If the required purchase quantity is two, the final price is per item, not the total cost for both items.

Column 8: Percentage saved off the full price after the coupons are deducted from the sale price. Although we do not show the full price due to space limitations, the final savings is calculated as compared to the item's full price, not its sale price. This gives shoppers an indication of whether or not the item is a good deal according to their price points, and gives them an idea of whether or not they should stock up on the item.

Notice that Hormel chili is listed twice, because there is both an Internet printable coupon and a newspaper coupon available for the item. This list also shows some items with coupons that expire before the advertised sale ends (the coupon for the Keebler cookies expires on 11/30, but the sale ends on 12/4). The Best-Deals List includes upcoming expiration dates to avoid any surprises at the register.

Shoppers will also be alerted if they can maximize their savings creatively by working with stores' savings policies. For example, the two shampoo brands listed are "buy one, get one free." At a specific store the shopper does need to buy two items to realize the savings, but the store allows the shopper to use two coupons with "buy one, get one free" offers. Therefore we remind shoppers of this opportunity and add it into the savings calculation.

The lists are formatted in an interactive format. Shoppers can sort the lists in any format they prefer. Or the list can be printed out as is.

The Best-Deals Lists for most cities are based on the advertised sale items in the store's weekly ad flyer. There may be slight variations in prices between stores in different cities within a chain, but even if the actual price varies by a few cents, the list will provide a good indication of which items matched with coupons are probably good deals.

Few of our Best-Deals Lists include unadvertised sale items because these can vary dramatically by individual store within the same city, which is frustrating for shoppers who carefully plan and organize their lists and coupons.

If an advertised sale item does not show a sale price in the store, check the store's actual ad flyer to confirm that it is on sale in that store (even weekly ad flyers can vary slightly within a city). If the item is on sale in the store's ad, show it to the cashier or manager so he or she honors the advertised price.

Also, if an advertised sale item is out of stock, go to the store's customer service counter to request a rain check—a piece of paper indicating the current sales price that you can use in a future week when the item is no longer on sale. This simple step can help save you money and frustration. The rain check may have an expiration date, but it's up to each store how long they honor rain checks.

The Best-Deals Lists on my website are updated on the day prices change. In rare cases the grocery chains may not have a weekly ad available (such as after a holiday), but the website will explain why there isn't a list.

> *"I use your site religiously every week and donate to charity every month. I save at least 55-60% every week on my own groceries. I have been able to stock up on our frequently used items at very low prices. I've not encountered a site like this before yours. I rarely, if ever, find any discrepancies in pricing, and the posting of the new week is like clockwork."*
>
> *~ Heather, Georgia*

Create Your List and Start Shopping

1. Determine which one or two stores you plan to use, based on what you learned in researching your stores' savings programs. If you are going to shop at only one store each week, select the store with the best prices on your highest-impact items that week.

2. Each week, review the weekly advertising circulars for your store(s) (either the actual ad or online). Begin your weekly meal planning with the sales ad. As much as possible, build your shopping list around what's on sale. If the store features any of your high-impact items at rock-bottom prices, be sure to stock up for a few weeks to avoid paying full price in future weeks. Check the store ad for any in-ad coupons, special promotions, or automatic rebates for your items.

3. Add other items you need to your list, and compare prices between the name-brand item and the store-brand item as you shop to determine the best value.

4. If your store price matches, look at other stores' ad circulars for low prices on items you need. If you find them, bring their ad along on your shopping trip to show the cashier the price to match for those items.

5. Check your coupon organization system (either Virtual Coupon Organizer or your own coupon organizer) to see if coupons are available for the items on your list.

6. Check the online coupon sites for any offers for the items you need, if in fact your stores accept printable coupons (*SmartSource.com*, *Eversave.com*, *CoolSavings.com*, *Boodle.com*, *Upons.com*).

7. Assemble your coupons, your shopping list, and any discount cards to make sure you have everything before you shop. Being organized will make it faster and easier at the register.

8. Bring your pocket coupon organizer to the store with coupons cut out for items you know you'll buy (if they go on sale). If you see good unadvertised sales in the store and have coupons available, you'll be able to take advantage of them. If you see good sales and realize you don't have those coupons with you, note the sale price and the date the sale ends (which may be printed on the shelf tag) so you can take advantage of the deal on your next shopping trip. Also check for in-store coupons located in the red coupon boxes on the shelves and on special displays.

9. As your items are rung up, watch the price of each item. It is common for prices to be incorrect in the system, and you can save quite a bit of money over the year by catching overcharges (the most common error is being charged the full price for a sale item whose price wasn't changed in the store's system). Also, watch as your coupons are scanned to be sure that they double when they should and that the cashier scans them all. Some stores offer a "price accuracy" guarantee, which gives the customer the item free if the price rings up incorrectly.

10. Don't forget to check the savings total at the bottom of your receipt—that's your performance review and compensation for your effort.

In the example below, this shopper saved a total of $75. If it took the shopper a full hour of planning and organizing (and it should take less time than that), I'd say $75 an hour is a respectable wage.

Total before coupons or discounts:	$125
Store club card savings:	$50
Manufacturers' coupon savings:	$25
Subtotal after sales and coupons:	$50
Total savings:	$75
Percentage saved:	60

As you can see from this receipt's data, it is possible to achieve dramatic savings on your grocery bill when you apply strategic-shopping methods. This shopper recognized rock-bottom sale prices (principle #1: Know your prices), took advantage of store promotions (principle #2: Know your store's savings programs), and had the right coupons (principle #3: Know your coupons). She saved a whopping 60 percent, slicing $75 from her total bill.

Now that you have these principles firmly under your belt, you can look forward to achieving these kinds of savings every week.

> *"I've cut my grocery bill by 48 percent on average! One week I saved a whopping 69% and couldn't believe how many bags of groceries I was walking out with for only $112. I used to spend that much but have next to nothing to show for it. And better yet, I buy really good deals in quantity and donate to our local women's shelter. Last week, I got great deals on Kleenex and snack foods that I donated to my children's school."*
>
> ~ *Michelle, Michigan*

My objective is to empower people to save the most money possible on their groceries by providing information and tools to plan their shopping trips efficiently and economically. I want to empower you!

The Best-Deals List will help you start saving immediately.

Chapter 5

Store Strategies and Supermarket Secrets

If you are new to the idea of using coupons and strategically saving money at the grocery store, you are starting at a great time. Since 2001 many stores have implemented highly automated savings programs, making it easy for busy shoppers to take advantage of great savings with little effort.

Creative manufacturers and marketers are introducing Internet-based programs that are easy to use. For example, in the past the only way shoppers could get lucrative rebates was by mailing in a form, proof-of-purchase seals, a register receipt, and possibly a stamped envelope. As a result, few shoppers took advantage of rebates. Today, if they know what to look for, shoppers can get rebates credited immediately on their grocery receipt or in a special savings account when they make a specific qualifying purchase. No paperwork involved at all!

I recall teaching a grocery-saving seminar a few years ago. Before I began a woman approached me and said, "I have been shopping with coupons for years. I doubt if you can tell me anything I don't already know." I wasn't sure how to respond, but proceeded to teach my seminar, which included many new automated savings programs. At the end of the seminar, the same woman came up to thank me, saying that she had learned about many programs that were new to her. The lesson: watch for new savings strategies, as today's marketers introduce new savings programs relatively quickly with the Internet.

As the comment below will testify, my website has made saving much easier for many shoppers. I am thrilled to share new information on how to save even more as marketers and retailers introduce new savings opportunities:

> *"Thank you very much for your site—the information has helped the two of us (senior citizens) a lot with our shopping. We don't have much money, but with coupons and the information from your site, we are able to get things for very little or free. We may not have much, but we manage, and it's nice to be able to help others."*

When I began my website five years ago, I had many years of couponing experience using traditional strategies to save on groceries. In the past five years the dynamics of grocery coupons, rebate programs, and store savings programs have changed rapidly—and are now far easier for shoppers to use. Thousands of coupon users visit my website each week, and they love to tell me about any new program or policy change. That keeps me up-to-date on new strategies and savings opportunities.

While tracking grocery prices, sale prices, and grocery coupons every week across the country to create Best-Deals Lists, I have learned how to find the best grocery deals at any store by understanding how pricing and promotional programs work. Every store chain's pricing works a little differently, and every store's coupon policies vary slightly. When we add a new store to our Best-Deals Lists, we have learned what questions to ask the store manager in order to determine where our site users can save the most money. The site shows new Best-Deals Lists every week at stores we've never even seen! It isn't difficult to find the deals—it's just a matter of knowing the rules and matching numbers.

If shoppers know what to look for and the questions to ask store personnel, they can learn how to stretch their hard-earned dollars at any store that sells groceries, in any city. Stick with me—a few details here may seem complex, but once you understand them you'll be on your way to saving thousands of dollars a year!

Every week thousands of items are on sale in a grocery store (the typical large supermarket has an average of twenty-two thousand items). Each week the larger cities' Sunday papers issue an average of a hundred grocery coupons, and some weeks almost two hundred. Sales and coupons are both examples of marketing strategies, and the companies who are the most active marketers typically employ several marketing strategies, or offers, to get the attention of shoppers.

Some food manufacturers are more progressive with marketing programs than others. These companies tend to provide offers in several locations in the store at the same time to attract shoppers. Fortunately these marketers are larger companies with household-name products. Remember, we don't have to stop buying our favorite brands to save money; we just learn to buy them differently.

Of the $709 billion that shoppers spent on food grown or raised on farms in 2002, the actual cost of the food (paid to the farmers) was $132.5 billion, or 19 percent of the total spent. The remaining 81 percent of our food dollar covers the labor, processing, packaging, storage, displaying, marketing, and advertising required to bring that food to consumers[1]. That suggests that we could each save close to 80 percent if we raised or grew all of our own food—a very hard job! I think I'll stick with strategic shopping. Believe it or not, some shoppers I know save 80 percent or more on their groceries, although saving 50 percent on average is more realistic.

Consider all your shopping options and your list of typical items purchased. You now know how to do specific price comparisons for typical supermarkets, discount stores, and wholesale clubs, as well as how to consider potential bargains available at nontraditional grocery sources (outlets, dollar stores, health-food stores, and farmers' markets). Each of these options can provide savings, depending on the items you buy, geographic convenience, membership club fees, and your ability to control impulse shopping. Once you determine which stores make sense for your household's shopping, you can zero in on how to make the most of each store's savings programs.

Studies show that the primary factor in influencing a shopper's choice of stores is location, location, location. Every shopper has different preferences, but I believe most people are too busy to make their shopping complicated. For most shoppers, simplifying the grocery-shopping process is as important as saving money. We shop at traditional supermarkets because they are convenient to where we live or work.

Even if you do some of your shopping at other stores, you need to know how to be a strategic shopper at major supermarkets if you want to save the most money. As I mentioned earlier, I personally find it most convenient to shop at my two closest supermarkets, usually alternating trips between the two stores. I might save a little more if I went to more stores to get their best deals, but the additional savings is not worth the extra travel time from my home. However, each shopper's time, geographic, and financial constraints are different, so everyone has to determine their best system.

Supermarkets have the most stores nationally, and most shoppers do at least some, if not all, of their shopping at their nearest supermarket. However, most shoppers are unaware of the many savings programs available to them, even in their own supermarkets. Simply understanding how to "work" the savings programs at your chosen store can dramatically cut your grocery bill. You just need to know the questions to ask to become an expert strategic shopper immediately.

In 2004 a television station in Michigan aired a story about my program; they sent a consumer reporter on a shopping trip with a local shopper to demonstrate my system. At the end of the trip, after the shopper saved over 70 percent on a large basket of groceries, the reporter said, "You've just made the supermarket a dollar store." We laughed at his comment, and realized that is exactly what she did!

Supermarket Savings Programs and Offers

Grocery stores use a variety of sale-pricing strategies. All traditional supermarkets feature weekly sale items. Stores using discount cards typically require customers to scan the card in order to receive sale prices. Food manufacturers give stores discount pricing that the stores pass on to shoppers.

Some sale items are featured in the store's sales ad, but most sale items are not in the weekly ad and are posted on the store shelf (referred to as "unadvertised sale items").

Sale items can be promoted in a number of ways, such as "Buy One, Get One Free" promotions, "Dollar Days," "10 for $10" and so on. When it comes to special promotions, knowing how your store actually prices these items at the register can make a real difference in increasing your savings.

Buy One, Get One Free (BOGO)

This very popular promotion can mean big savings for smart shoppers. Although many stores charge full price for the first item purchased, and give the second item to shoppers free, some stores actually charge half price for each "buy one, get one free" item, meaning the shopper only has to buy one item to realize the savings.

Knowing how your store charges for BOGO promotions can help you save. For example, if the average shopper saw that her two supermarkets, store A and store B, both featured a "buy one, get one free" promotion on the same cereal for $4, they would probably think the cereals were the same price at each store. However, store B actually had the better price. The following examples demonstrate why.

Store A BOGO Policy	Charges full price for the first item and zero for the second; must buy two items to realize the savings.
Coupon Policy	Doubles coupons up to 50 cents.
Cost of Item 1	Cereal at $4 is Buy One Get One Free. First item is $4.
Cost of Item 2	Second item is $0.
Shopper's Best Deal	Buy two items; use one coupon which is doubled. $4 less $0.50 / 2 = $3 for two boxes cereal.
Final Cost	$1.50 per box of cereal.

Store B BOGO Policy	Charges half price for each item; only need to buy one item to realize the savings.
Coupon Policy	Doubles coupons up to 50 cents.
Cost of Item 1	Cereal at $4 is Buy One Get One Free. First item is $2.
Cost of Item 2	Second item is $0.
Shopper's Best Deal	Buy 1 item and use one coupon which is doubled. $2 less $0.50 / 2 = $1 for one box cereal.
Final Cost	$1 for one box of cereal.

Assume you have a coupon for 50 cents off one box of this cereal, and both store A and store B double coupons. Even though their cereal offer is the same price and their double-coupon policy is the same, you would save more by buying store B's deal simply by understanding how they charge for "Buy One, Get One Free" offers.

Multiple-Purchase Pricing Promotions

Many stores set sale pricing to encourage the purchase of multiple items. For example, a store would commonly display a sign, "Three for $6." It is important to know whether or not that store charges $2 for each item, or whether shoppers must buy three items to benefit from the sale price.

Most stores charge individually per item even though their signs lead you to believe you need to buy multiple items. This is one more example of good merchandising by the store. There are exceptions, so verify your stores' policies. Stores that require multiple purchases to get the sale price usually indicate that stipulation clearly in their store ad and on shelf price tags.

Retailers commonly show examples of coupon savings in the Sunday newspaper coupon circulars, which demonstrate the final price and savings that would result from using the coupon. However, many times the calculation assumes that shoppers will buy multiple items, even if the coupon or the store's pricing does not require multiple purchases.

This is an advertiser's example of a good coupon deal:

Hormel Chili:

Sale Price	Two for $2
Coupon	50 cents
Double cpn	50 cents
Final Price:	Two for $1, or 50 cents/can

This store actually charges $1 for each can, but the shopper is not required to buy two cans to realize the savings.

Here is the real savings story:

Hormel Chili:

Sale Price	$1
Coupon	50 cents
Double cpn	50 cents
Final Price:	Free

Now that's better. Once you know the store's pricing practices, you will pay the lowest prices on your groceries.

Weekly Advertising Circulars
With Featured Sale Items

Planning your shopping trip is critical to reducing your grocery spending, so the weekly ads are a strategic shopper's first resource for finding grocery deals. Today many grocery and drugstores make their weekly ads available online, so if you do not get your ad in the mail or delivered with your newspaper you can check out the sales online before you go to the store. Weekly ads usually feature the best sale items on the front and back pages, and may even feature popular items at prices below their cost to attract shoppers. These loss leaders are the first deals we look for each week. Loss-leader prices are your starting point, so if coupons are available for the same items, you will really save.

Loss-leader items tend to be common items that are generally perishable or require more storage space so they are difficult for shoppers to stockpile. They may also have purchase limits (such as "limit four") or minimum purchase requirements (such as "with a $10 minimum order"). Common loss-leader items are milk, eggs, bread, flour, soft drinks, and produce. They attract shoppers to the store, and are probably located in the back of the store, requiring the shopper to walk through other departments on their way to find the item, encouraging impulse purchases.

Shoppers may find higher-priced, complementary items located near loss leaders or featured items. For example, a cake mix priced at a rock-bottom price may have full-priced frosting included in the display. Featured produce may have full-priced salad dressings near the display. Additional sales of higher-priced items justify the low-priced loss leaders for the store's overall profits. However, strategic shoppers wait to buy these additional items when they are on sale and when they have a coupon for them too.

When you try to reduce grocery spending, you will save the most by planning your week's meals around what is on sale in the flyer (or what you've purchased in past weeks on sale). If you find you haven't been able to plan and organize before you shop, at least pick up the store flyer when you arrive at the store to take advantage of sale and loss-leader items easily. Even a small amount of planning will help you save money.

Although weekly sales flyers feature many items, you cannot assume that all of the featured "sale prices" are always the best bargains. Over the course of a few months, the same item's price can fluctuate dramatically, and the stores may promote a "sale price" with a special sale tag anytime the item is less than full price, even if it is only a few cents less.

Once you begin paying attention and tracking the price points of your most frequently purchased items, you will easily recognize true bargains and know when to take advantage by stocking up. You may find your items' sale prices fall to 50 percent off their full prices or more, and having a coupon can lower those prices to 80 percent or more off the full price. My Best-Deals List will quickly tell you the savings percentage off the store's regular price for each deal to make bargains easy to spot.

Price-Matching Policies

Some stores guarantee to honor the lowest price in the market, and will "match" other stores' advertised sale prices if the customer brings the ad to the store to prove that a lower price is available that week for the same item. Using the "price matching" strategy can save shoppers the time of going to several stores to buy the lowest-priced sale items at each one.

Price-Accuracy Guarantees

Stores guarantee that the prices rung up at the register will be accurate and there are scanner laws in some states that protect against scanner fraud. Some stores will give you, the customer, the item free if you alert them to the problem. For example, an item may be listed as $3 in the store ad, but the register may charge $4. If you watch the prices at the register and notice a discrepancy, stores with accuracy guarantees deduct the $4 charge, enter the correct price and then give you the item free too.

Even if your store does not have this guarantee, you should watch the prices as your items are rung in at the register. It is not unusual for errors to happen, particularly on sale items. If the price hasn't been changed in the system to reflect the sale price, you may be overcharged accidentally. Don't feel embarrassed to point these errors out to the store, because once the price is corrected in the system, you are helping other shoppers.

Bonus Coupon Policies

Many grocery stores attract coupon shoppers by doubling or tripling the face value of manufacturers' coupons every day (an example of a store "doubling a coupon" would be taking $1 off your order when you use a 50-cent coupon). In a recent industry survey, 46 percent of grocery stores surveyed offer double- or triple-coupon policies[2]. According to the July 2004 CMS Marketing Insights' Bonus Coupon Study, stores are more likely to double coupons than triple them, and coupon doubling tends to be more common in certain parts of the country where competition is more intense among retailers. You can find a complete list of retailers' coupon policies and more interesting coupon facts at *CouponInfoNow.com*.

The bonus coupon policy of your store is key to saving money on groceries. My two supermarkets both double coupons every day and have for years. I am amazed at how often regular shoppers of these stores ask me, "Which day of the week does store X double coupons?" There are signs all over the store and in their ads promoting their daily double coupon policy! All you have to do is pay attention.

I've done consumer-shopping television news stories in many states.

All I did to prepare for the stories was to use the Best-Deals Lists on my website along with the required coupons for those best deals. When I arrived at each city's airport, I went straight to the store, easily found the items, and purchased them for next to nothing because the stores had great double-coupon policies. In one case, I bought $112 worth of groceries for $1.95, and other shoppers were amazed. I told them, "I don't even live here. You could be doing this every week; it's easy!" It's simply a matter of matching featured sale items with coupons from the newspaper each week, and knowing which stores have the best coupon policies. Of course, I had the advantage of following the website deals list, which had already done the research for me, but anyone can do that.

Electronic Discounts

Manufacturers also work with grocery stores to offer special promotions to encourage shoppers to buy multiple items in exchange for additional discounts deducted automatically, or electronically, at the register.

A typical example of a promotion would be to reward a shopper with a free gallon of milk if the shopper buys four boxes of a particular brand of cereal. Another recent offer rewarded shoppers with two cartons of ice cream if they purchased twelve frozen diet entrees. (Pretty ironic, isn't it?) These promotions are easy for the shopper because they are tracked automatically, and the discount is taken off of the total with no effort by the shopper.

Promotion details are typically explained in the store sales flyer or on a sign posted near the qualifying product. Look for these promotions, because you can miss out on big savings if you purchase qualifying items (especially if you buy slightly less than the amount required to get the bonus). I remember seeing a woman in the grocery store buying qualifying items. She put ten of them in her cart, but she only needed to buy two more to have $6 automatically deducted from her bill. The additional two items cost an additional $4. If she hadn't been standing next to an obsessed strategic shopper, she would have missed out on the savings entirely because she hadn't read the weekly ad.

Shopper Rewards Programs

The Internet has enabled food manufacturers to attract shoppers with automatic rewards programs such as Upromise. The Upromise program rewards shoppers (who are members of this free program) with a cash rebate of up to 5 percent of their grocery purchases on specific brands. This is literally free money if you are already buying the participating products. This rebate is then put into a college savings account that is controlled by the member. The program appeals to parents with children at home—the largest group of grocery spenders. Not surprisingly, participating products are geared to parents as well (diapers, baby foods, cereals, and hundreds of other common grocery items).

You can also find a full list of participating products on the Upromise website at *Upromise.com*. Shoppers simply sign up for a free Upromise account and enter their store's discount card number to have rebates tracked automatically. Shoppers do not have to track their purchases or mail in any information to get credit—it is all done automatically when they use their store discount card on every shopping trip.

Quarterly statements of savings accumulated are also available on the Upromise website. If you are not already a member, go to *Upromise.com* to begin taking advantage of free money. If you are a member, be sure to check that your current store discount card is entered in your profile.

Finally, you can solicit relatives to join the program and have them designate your child as the beneficiary to save even more. I spoke with one smart grocery store manager who had eighteen relatives join Upromise and designate his son as the beneficiary!

Grocery Rebate Credit Cards

Some grocery stores have partnered with banks to provide rebate credit cards, rewarding shoppers with a percentage of their grocery spending as well as other purchases made with the card. Rebate percentages on grocery spending tend to be the highest, and some retailers even give a higher rebate on the purchases of their own store brands.

Programs to Benefit Charities and Schools

Many stores provide special cards or membership programs to allow shoppers to designate a school or charity to receive a donation from the store as a percentage of the shopper's spending. This does not cost the shopper any extra money. Some stores also participate in the national "Box Tops for Education" or "Campbell's Labels for Education" programs, which allow shoppers to help increase donations to their local schools. Check with your store's customer service personnel for details. It can be easy and free for shoppers to help fund their favorite charities and/or schools if they take advantage of the community programs offered by their stores.

If a store participates in the Upromise program or a rebate credit card, they will have information about the programs at their customer-service counter. Check with your store's personnel.

Combining Offers—True Strategic Shopping

"Your website has saved me a ton of money. Last Sunday's trip to the grocery store was my best yet. My total before my savings

card and coupons was $140 and afterwards it was $70, plus I got a $5 gift certificate to use at my next shopping trip. Plus I have receipts to send in for my $10 rebate check for buying three Pepsi products and bags of chips.

"So really, including all the rebates and special offers, I only spent $55, which is a savings of $85. I can't thank you enough. I bought eight boxes of oatmeal for $4 all together. They were BOGO free plus I had three $1 off coupons plus one $.50 coupon doubled. Safeway also had the deal where you get $5 off automatically if you buy any eight Quaker products, so I got eight boxes for less than I would usually pay for one box!"

~ Alaina

Once you know how these offers work, you can see how combining them at a store that offers the most attractive programs can really help you save. "Buy one, get one free" offers are a typical example of a deal found regularly at supermarkets.

Here is an example: brand-name cake mix is "buy one, get one free." Regularly $1.90 per box, this store charges half price for each item (95 cents per box). You have a newspaper coupon available for 35 cents per box. This store doubles coupons up to 50 cents. Result: Buy each box for 95 cents, with the 35-cent doubled coupon (95 cents less 70 cents), so you pay 25 cents per box, a savings of 87 percent off the regular price.

In addition, 2 percent of the purchase price goes into your Upromise college savings account. A percentage of the purchase price goes to your child's school. Then you can cut off the cake-mix box top, turn it in to the school, and the school will get 10 cents.

What a deal!

"I love the Coupon Mom website! I have learned how to greatly reduce my grocery bill and help others at the same time. A few years ago I was working part-time when I found out about serious

couponing. This means matching items on sale with coupons to get those items for free or cheap. By saving so much money on my grocery bill, I was able to quit work and stay at home with the kids. Some people pay between $500 and $1,000 a month for groceries. I usually pay between $150 and $250. That savings has allowed me to be home when my kids get home from school. It also has allowed us to afford other things that we would have had to put off. When my kids want a certain brand of shoes I can now afford to get them.

"I have also learned that when something is going to be free with coupon, buy it! Even if you are not going to use it, someone else will benefit. I found a local food bank that loves getting my freebies. Living in the area I do, some people think that there is no need for a food bank. But many of the people that benefit from it are single moms that have a hard time making their dollar stretch. It is my pleasure to help any way I can.

"I am always telling my friends about how much money I have saved. Some think it takes too much time, while others are slowly coming around. My kids even know not to ask for something at the store unless it is on sale and we have a coupon. My theory is you work hard for that dollar, make it work for you!"

~ *Laura, California*

Chapter 6

The Right Questions
Equal Big Savings

Because every store has its own set of promotions and their own methods for implementing them, strategic shoppers learn how their stores' programs work in order to save the most money. You can begin saving immediately by knowing what questions to ask your store personnel.

Store Sales-Policy Questions

1. *When you have a "buy one, get one free" offer (BOGO), is each item charged half price or is the first item charged full price and the second item charged at zero?*

As our $4 BOGO cereal example in chapter 5 showed, when shoppers know exactly how their stores' policies work, they can pay less for BOGO deals when they combine them with coupons. When a store charges half price for each BOGO item, the shopper can buy just one item if that's all she needs. And by using a coupon on the one half-price item, she pays the lowest possible price for the item.

If the store charges full price for the first item and zero for the second item, then the smart shopper would always get both items. If the shopper only bought one item, he or she would pay the same price for one item as the shopper who remembered to pick up the free second item.

2. Can I use two coupons with a "buy one, get one free" offer?

Some stores will allow shoppers to use two coupons with their BOGO deals. Knowing this policy can help coupon users save twice as much if they have more than one coupon for the same item.

3. Do you have to use a store discount card? Are there any special advantages or promotions available for card members?

Many stores have a frequent shopper card, also referred to as a store discount card or a club card. Although some shoppers complain that they don't like to have their purchases tracked and monitored, the reality is, shoppers tend to get more relevant promotional information and offers as a result of being a card member.

For example, if a card member routinely purchases specific items, that member may receive a coupon for those items or something similar. The cost of producing and mailing direct mail pieces is expensive, so advertisers are much more effective at attracting shoppers with targeted offers if they know what items shoppers prefer. As a result, they send more specific offers to smaller groups of shoppers. If you receive a mailing from your supermarket, be sure to open it because it will probably have an offer you like!

Some supermarkets have negotiated special offers with local businesses on behalf of their card members. You can check your supermarkets' websites or ask their customer-service personnel to see what offers are available in your area.

Finally, if your supermarket has a club card or discount card program and you do not want to use it, you would be wise to find a supermarket that does not require the use of a discount card to get sale prices and coupon bonuses. If non-card-users shop at discount-card stores, they will spend far more money than necessary.

4. *Do you match the sale prices of other stores? Do you accept in-ad coupons from competitors' sales flyers?*

Some stores will "price match," meaning they will match the sales price of a competitor's store if you bring in the competitor's ad flyer. For example, if your store's competitor has a particular brand of cereal on sale ($2 per box) and you have a coupon for $1 off that same item, which is selling for $4 per box at your store, you could have the store price match the competitor's sale price of $2 and use the $1 coupon to get the cereal for $1 per box rather than $3 per box (your store's current price of $4 less your $1 coupon).

Another example: Your store has that cereal on sale for $2, and the competitor's store has an in-ad coupon for $1 off that brand in its store. If your store accepted competitor coupons, you could combine the sale price with the coupon and get $1 off of the $2 sale price, paying only $1 per box.

Store Coupon-Policy Questions

Simply knowing each store's policy on competitors' pricing and coupons can help you save money without making several shopping trips. What is your coupon policy? Does your store double or triple the face value of coupons? Up to what amount? In addition to these obvious questions, you'll come up with your own that will relate to your shopping and store needs.

Example of a store that doubles coupons up to 50 cents: Campbell's Select soup is on sale for $1, and you have a coupon for 50 cents. The register deducts 50 cents from the manufacturer's coupon and an additional 50 cents to double the coupon's value. Total cost to the shopper: $1 minus $1 (50 cents + 50 cents) = zero, or free. The food manufacturer reimburses the store 50 cents for the face value of the coupon, plus an additional amount for coupon processing. The store pays the cost of the doubled portion (50 cents, in this case).

Double- and triple-coupon policies vary across the country. Some store chains choose not to double coupons, but they accept expired coupons instead. The most common coupon policy is to double coupons up to 50 cents (to a maximum total of $1 off), although a few states have stores that double coupons up to $1 (to a total of $2 off) every day.

1. *Is there a limit on the number of coupons that can be doubled for multiple, identical items?*

Here's an example of a store that doubles coupons but limits the number of multiple coupons: You have three cans of Campbell's Select soup and three coupons, one for each can of soup. The soup is on sale for $1; the coupons are for 50 cents per can. The store doubles the first two coupons for multiple identical items, and deducts only the face value of the coupon for any additional identical items.

Soup #1: $1 less 50-cent coupon. Doubled = $1 less $1 = free

Soup #2: $1 less 50-cent coupon. Doubled = $1 less $1 = free

Soup #3: $1 less 50-cent coupon. Face value = $1 less 50 cents = 50 cents

If you didn't know your store's policy and you planned to buy several cans of soup with multiple coupons, you would pay more than you expected. Maximize your savings by knowing your store's limits and work within them. In this case, I would buy two cans with two coupons per trip to the store, or have my children buy their own order of two cans of soup to donate to charity. They are shoppers too!

2. Do you have special coupon bonus promotions during the year?

These promotions could be super-double or even triple-coupon week. You want to know how the store lets shoppers know about these promotions. Not all stores double or triple coupons every day, but they may choose to do so as a temporary promotion. Additionally, stores that double coupons up to 50 cents may announce "super double coupon days" where they double coupons up to $1 for a few days or a week. Experienced coupon users stay tuned to news of special promotions and stock up on deals at rock-bottom prices. Always check your store's ad circular or website for special coupon bonus promotions.

3. Do you accept expired coupons?

Stores that do not double or triple coupons may accept expired coupons as their promotional tool to attract coupon shoppers. This can be especially attractive, because manufacturers sometimes alternate their coupons and sales prices. For example, the price of a specific brand of cereal may hit its rock-bottom price after the coupon has expired (pur-posely timed). If you still had that coupon, you could really save.

4. Do you accept coupons printed on a home computer?

Printable Internet coupons are found at specific websites, including food manufacturers' sites and coupon sites like *Coolsavings.com, SmartSource.com, Boodle.com,* and *Eversave.com.* It is important to know if your store accepts coupons printed off a home computer to maximize your savings and avoid printing coupons unnecessarily. At the time of this writing, a small percentage of retailers do not accept them because of a coupon counterfeiting scam in August 2003.

Although those counterfeit coupons were completely different than those from the legitimate Internet sites, some retailers elected to discontinue accepting all coupons printed from a home computer.

5. Does your store offer Catalina coupons?

The store's system automatically generates coupons (typically at the checkout) for specific items or cash off your next order, based on items you purchase. These are called Catalina coupons. You will find special shelf tags next to qualifying items that describe the Catalina offer for that item (such as, if you buy two bottles of ketchup, you receive a coupon for $1 off ground beef).

6. Does your store have in-ad coupons that can be combined with manufacturers' coupons?

Many stores have coupons in their weekly ad flyer. The coupon may specify a promotion (such as "buy one, get one free") or a cash amount to be deducted (such as $1 off). The coupon will typically be labeled as either a "store coupon" or a "manufacturer's coupon." That distinction is important. Read on.

You can usually use both a store coupon and a manufacturer's coupon together on one item. Therefore if the weekly ad flyer had an in-ad coupon for $1 off a particular brand of cereal, and you also had a manufacturer's coupon for $1 off that cereal from the Sunday newspaper (or any other source), you would be able to use both of the coupons on the same box of cereal, saving a total of $2.

However, stores do not accept two manufacturer's coupons together for one item. Therefore it is important to look at the coupon in the weekly ad flyer to see if it says "manufacturer's coupon" at the top of the coupon. If so, use the coupon with the highest value if you want the item. If the coupon says "store coupon," you are in luck, and you can maximize your savings by using both coupons.

7. Does your store offer senior discounts on a particular day of the week?

This program is available at many stores, but shoppers may need to ask for the discount. For example, both of my supermarkets offer a 5 percent discount on Wednesdays, and age requirements vary by store. Over the course of a year, this additional savings can add up.

8. Does your store have a baby club that rewards shoppers with cash or merchandise?

Many supermarkets offer a program that gives bonus rewards on baby products, based on qualifying spending. The programs may also include regular mailings with coupons for diapers, formula, baby food, and other baby products. Some programs give double the reward credit when shoppers purchase the store-brand item. A typical reward could be $10 on $200 of products purchased, or $10 on $100 of store-brand products purchased. Ultimately you could stock up on name-brand diapers when they are offered on sale, use coupons available, get baby-club credit, and also receive a contribution in your Upromise account. Or you could wait for the store-brand diaper to go on sale, then stock up and get double the reward credits in the store's baby club. (If your child outgrows the size you stocked up on, most stores will exchange an unopened package of diapers for the next size up.)

9. Does your store have a store magazine or newsletter that includes coupons available to subscribers?

Many grocery stores publish their own magazine with recipes, health information, and coupons. The magazines are probably available at the customer-service desk or in a special rack for brochures and flyers at the front of the store. If you pick up a magazine, be sure to subscribe to home delivery. Stores' magazines mailed to your home are more likely to include coupons than the ones available in the store.

10. *Does your store have any additional frequent shopper programs you should know about (such as a film-developing club, Starbucks coffee club, Fresh Express salad club, prescription transfer program, pet club, or wine club)?*

You can find out about specific reward programs by asking at the customer-service desk or asking the manager for that particular store department.

11. Does your store offer an email newsletter with store coupons and special offers?

Be sure to check your store's website to take advantage of email newsletters. Examples of offers I've seen in email newsletters include a weekly coupon to buy a specified item for one cent, coupons to use for online shopping at that store, and special offers from grocery manufacturers or other business partners.

12. *How extensive is your line of store-brand items?*

Larger supermarket chains offer comprehensive lines of store-brand items. I like to purchase store-brand alternatives for my key items when the name brand is not on sale with a coupon. Store brands now include several quality levels, offering premium options as well as basic, bargain items. These days you can even find complete lines of organic and health-food options in store brands. In many cases the same companies that package and sell name-brand counterparts provide the products sold under the store's private label, so you aren't sacrificing quality when you buy store-brand items.

13. *Does your store have a quality guarantee for its store-brand items?*

Some stores offer a "try it, like it, or get the national brand free" guarantee, which makes trying store-brand items a no-brainer. I like that guarantee because I do not risk wasting my money trying new items. I can always return the store-brand item if it is unsatisfactory and get the name-brand item I prefer.

Chapter 7

Virtual Coupon Organizer to the Rescue!

Imagine you went to the public library to find a specific book. Even though the library is filled with thousands of books, you can find what you're looking for easily by using the online catalog. You get the book and take it home to read for a few weeks at no charge. What a great system!

Now, imagine how difficult it would be to locate the book you needed, out of thousands of books, if there was no online catalog or shelving system to organize them? How long would it take to search the shelves to find one book? Most likely you would stop using the library if the place wasn't organized. You would miss out on a wonderful resource because you couldn't find anything easily.

You know where I'm going with this. That is exactly how dealing with grocery coupons is for most people. When you look through the Sunday newspaper coupon circular, the coupons are in no particular order (not alphabetized, not in order of food category) and they are printed in many different sizes. Some coupons are so large they need to be folded in half in an organizer, and other coupons are so small you may not even be able to spot them as you glance through the circular quickly. The expiration dates can be located in various spots on the coupon, and some expiration dates are so small they are almost impossible to read.

Only about 15 percent of shoppers use coupons every single week, but about 69 percent of shoppers do use coupons occasionally[1]. That suggests that more people would be willing to use coupons if they were easier to use. I figured there had to be a solution, so I came up with one.

The Virtual Coupon Organizer™ (VCO) is the most useful tool for any shopper to save money on groceries—in any city. I think of it as the Dewey decimal system of grocery coupons. It literally organizes the information of thousands of grocery coupons to make it easy for shoppers to find the coupons they need. Best of all, you do not have to be a perfectly disciplined coupon user to save big money when you have the VCO to help you. As long as you put aside the weekly Sunday newspaper coupon circular (no need to cut anything out) the VCO will work for you. Whether several times a week or only once a year, you'll save money when you use the VCO. It gives shoppers unlimited possibilities to save money with coupons.

I had an opportunity to teach third graders how to buy food for charity with coupons in creating my Kids Cut Out Hunger program. The teacher suggested the idea of putting the date on the cover of the coupon circular and then referencing the coupon date next to each grocery deal on the Best-Deals List. Students would only have to cut out the few coupons they needed by finding the dated coupon circular, which is much easier than cutting out and organizing one hundred to two hundred coupons a week.

I finally had the answer to my question of how to keep track of all those circulars. But how would I find someone or something to make my vision a reality.

I approached some Georgia Tech students, who agreed to develop a more-efficient software system for my website, as their senior project. They immediately recognized the potential of automating the maintenance of my coupon database, as well as giving site users the ability to access it.

I knew that they were onto something big because even coupon-averse shoppers would be able to save money if they had access to the coupon database I used. They could just save the circular and put the date on the front of it. When they needed particular coupons, they simply cut out only the ones they needed. This would save hours of time a month for frequent coupon users! Most importantly it could help even the busiest person become a consistent coupon user, saving the most money possible in the least amount of time.

Being able to provide the Virtual Coupon Organizer to the public could dramatically change the way shoppers used coupons, and could easily increase the number of successful coupon users and food donors.

After the launch of the Virtual Coupon Organizer, I began to hear from people who had never wanted to use coupons in the past but decided to give coupons a try with this new system. Many shoppers let me know they were saving money with coupons for the first time, and donating food to charity too.

> *"I am the wife of an army reserve soldier deployed to Iraq last year. I saw a news story about your site and have used coupons for years with varying success. It was getting difficult to spend the time sorting through all the coupons while maintaining our small ranch, working part-time, caring for our children and sending nightly emails and weekly letters to my husband in the war zone. I shop at Kroger and Brookshires in Texas and find your site very easy to use. My best day was a 75 percent savings. I average about 30 percent to 40 percent savings. I can easily pick up non-*

perishables for pennies or for free and donate them through my church to the local food pantry. I also have started donating items at Kroger to their red-barrel program when I find a bargain there. I think what you are doing is great and I have told others struggling with the budget setbacks of being an active reserve family how to stretch their food dollars too. Many active duty families live close to a base where they can shop at the commissary, discounted about 15 to 20 percent. But we reservists are sprinkled throughout the countryside and are often far from these stores."

~ Sue, Texas

Introducing the Virtual Coupon Organizer proved it could help us reach far more shoppers and help convert all those discarded grocery coupons ($315 billion, remember?) into real cash for many people.

Although the Sunday newspaper coupons are produced by the same two companies every week (SmartSource and Valassis), different versions of the circulars with varying offers are issued across the country—more than two hundred different versions of the circulars in fifty states. Both national and regional advertisers issue coupons in these circulars, so they can vary quite a bit across the country.

Using the Virtual Coupon Organizer

Here are all the ways you can use the Virtual Coupon Organizer (VCO) to maximize the value of your grocery coupons:

1. To use a library of coupon circulars, you obviously need to begin collecting them. You'll save more money if you have more than one copy of the coupon circular. You'll be able to take advantage of multiple coupons with this easy system.

Simply write the date and the first letter of the circular's name prominently on the front (such as 11/14V for November 14 in the Valassis circular, or 10/7S for October 7 in the SmartSource circular). Currently only the SmartSource and Valassis coupon circulars are included in the VCO for most markets. If you forget to write the circular date on the front, you can locate the date and the circular's newspaper in tiny print on the spine of the circular.

You can use the VCO as your only coupon organization system or combine it with a small coupon organizer. For example, what works best for me is to use a plastic coupon or check organizer. I label each section based on food categories and cut out some coupons for items I always tend to buy. That way they are on hand if I see a great unadvertised sale item when I'm shopping.

When I create my weekly shopping list from the Best-Deals List, I compile all of my coupons before each shopping trip. I keep the list and coupons in the front pocket of the organizer to make it easy to pay at the register. The small organizer also makes it easy to save coupons I receive from other sources, such as direct-mail pieces, in-store displays, magazines, and so on.

2. After you cut out the coupons you know you'll use, be sure to SAVE THE ENTIRE CIRCULAR. This is important. People tell me they don't use most of the items featured in the coupon circulars. However, when the item goes on sale a few weeks after the coupon has been issued, the coupon may make that item free. If it was a useful item for charity, wouldn't it make sense to pick up the item and donate it to a local food drive or food pantry at no cost to you? If you throw away 80 percent of the coupons, you will most likely miss out on many good charity items that could help people in your community.

With one hundred to two hundred coupons each Sunday, it is easy to overlook some as you review the circulars. Using the VCO and the Best-

Deals Lists makes it easy to view all the coupon offers and to be generous to your community with little time or money invested.

3. The new coupons listed in the VCO are available for shoppers to view the day they are available in the stores (the Saturday prior to that Sunday's paper). If you do not have a newspaper delivered, you can see which coupons will come out that day to determine if it makes sense to buy an extra copy of the paper. The VCO is automatically sorted by the date the coupon is issued, with the most recent week listed at the top. This makes it easier to see which coupons are new, which is particularly helpful if you are just starting your coupon collection.

4. The VCO describes exactly what items are included in the coupon offer. Many times shoppers will see the pictured item on the coupon and assume they must buy the exact variety pictured. However, the written coupon description determines how the coupon can be used. It is not unusual for the manufacturer to picture the most expensive variety of a product, while the wording of the coupon may say, "$1 off any variety." You will pay the lowest price if you use the coupon on the least expensive variety. When shoppers can read the written descriptions of each coupon in the VCO, they are more likely to use the coupon accurately and to their best advantage.

5. The database automatically deletes expired coupons, and the expiration date of the coupon is included in the VCO. You can sort the VCO by expiration dates to see which coupons expire in the upcoming week to make sure you take advantage of good offers for items you need.

6. You can use the VCO to create your own Best-Deals List at any store using the store's weekly ad flyer. Simply alphabetize the coupon list, note sale items you need in the ad, and check to see if a coupon for that item is available. If you can't find the coupon alphabetically, enter one word from the item description in the Search box on the VCO to see if

the coupon is listed under a different name. For example, you may be looking for a Pop Secret popcorn coupon and can't find it in the VCO. If you enter the word "popcorn" in the Search box, you may find that it is listed under "Betty Crocker Pop Secret Popcorn."

7. You can use the VCO to find coupons for items you need that are not in the store's sale flyer. For example, you may need ice cream. Enter the words "ice cream" in the Search box and it will show you a list of every unexpired coupon for any brand of ice cream.

8. You may be shopping at a store that does not have a weekly sales flyer, but you expect their everyday low prices when matched with coupons to be good deals (such as Super Target, Super Wal-Mart or some wholesale clubs that accept coupons). In that case, simply make your own shopping list based on what you know you need, and then search the VCO either alphabetically or by using the Search box to find coupons.

9. You do not have to be a disciplined or a regular coupon user to save money with the VCO. You can use the system once a week, once a month, or even once a year without keeping up with weekly coupon cutting and organizing. All you have to do is remember to put aside and label the coupon circulars each week. Even if you only have time to take advantage of coupons once in a while, it is possible to use the VCO to create your shopping list, find the coupons you need easily, and save a significant amount of money.

> "Using the CouponMom.com site has increased my ability to purchase grocery items at a significantly reduced cost without a lot of effort.

> "In the past, I would cut all my coupons apart and attempt to sort them in various food groups. While this worked to some degree in saving money, I was not able to effectively compare gro-

cery store sales with the coupons, and a lot of times I allowed coupons to expire for items that I really used on an ongoing basis.

"All of this changed when I started visiting CouponMom.com. I'm able to compare grocery ads with my coupons, only cutting out the coupons that I need for that one trip. I then walk into the store, get my items, and walk out using very little effort and time. Without the Coupon Mom my savings were about 20 percent, but with her method my savings have gone up to 70 to 75 percent.

"When my church's singles group decided to sponsor several food drives for missions, I encouraged individuals to donate their coupons to this effort so that we could purchase as much food for as little money as possible. This changed numerous lives in more ways than ever. We sent hundreds of pounds of food and personal items to areas in West Virginia, filling up U-hauls on each trip.

"When I travel to my parents' home in the Baton Rouge, Louisiana area, I am also able to use the Virtual Coupon Organizer for stores in Louisiana. It may sound crazy to go shopping in this fashion in another state but with this method I would be a fool NOT to buy as much food as possible for as little as possible—even if it is shopping in another state.

"Also, a great advantage of the Virtual Coupon Organizer is that I can sort coupons by expiration dates. This makes my coupon "loss" from expiration much less than it was in the past. I can find coupons that are expiring and stockpile or buy at other non-advertised stores, as needed.

"Even for those who do not use coupons, the site is a great blessing. Charitable food deals are listed specifically, making it very easy to point out sales that will benefit others."

~ Cecilia, Georgia

Chapter 8

The Twenty Best Places
to Find Grocery Coupons

I'll never forget going shopping at my store during super double-coupon week a few years ago (mind you this only happens about once every two years). I had a cart overflowing with groceries, with a coupon for every item, and was expecting to save 90 percent on my total bill. Orders like these usually take some time for the cashier to scan, deduct coupons, and call the manager over to request that he override the cash register's system.

As the cashier began ringing up my items, a man entered the line behind me. He had one item in his cart. I smiled politely and said, "I'm probably not the best person to stand behind because I have a lot of coupons." He smiled back and said nicely, "That's alright, I'm not in a hurry."

At least I warned him. I kept smiling at him, shrugging, and apologizing. His polite smile faded noticeably as time passed. I don't know how much longer it was before I finished my order, quite awhile I'm sure. As I happily rolled my cart toward the door, his order rang up quickly, and I heard the cashier ask him, "And do you have any coupons today?" His response still rings in my ears: "I should say not!"

The lesson: In a checkout line you don't want to be behind a strategic shopper. You want to be the strategic shopper—the one saving all the money—it's more fun.

Coupons are money. Period. Specifically, coupons for items that you use regularly are as good as money. You buy the product, you hand the cashier a piece of paper called a coupon, and they take $1 off your bill. That's currency, plain and simple.

Because it's a form of currency, I have great respect for coupons. I wouldn't throw dollar bills away, and I'm not likely to throw away $1 coupons for items I buy. If you are not a coupon user now, changing your perspective about coupons is a good first step toward saving big money.

Last year a TV station in my area filmed a news story about Cut Out Hunger and my website. The cameraman was creative, and he thought it would be funny if I sat on my office floor surrounded by coupons. I had a plastic box filled with my coupon circulars, which I used every week. He grabbed a handful to throw on the floor, and I flew across the room to grab them out of his hand. I said, "Wait, let me get some expired coupons!" He looked at me like I was a little off my rocker, but he hadn't seen the website demonstration yet. He had no idea how much money he had in his hand! He definitely wasn't a coupon user.

One of the most-important tools available to grocery shoppers is coupons. Fortunately there is no shortage of available free grocery coupons. In fact, 98 percent of the 342 billion coupons issued each year (worth $318 billion) are thrown away, primarily because they can be difficult to organize and use. As you know by now, my goal is to make it much easier for you to organize and know when to use coupons to help you take advantage of this significant financial resource. Coupons are real money when redeemed, so if you are throwing away coupons for items you currently buy, you are throwing away real money.

Sunday Circulars

The primary source for manufacturers' coupons is the Sunday newspaper coupon circular (provided by SmartSource and Valassis, as we've noted previously). Of the 342 billion manufacturers coupons distributed in 2004, 82 percent of them were found in the Sunday coupon circulars[1]. If you are new to couponing and overwhelmed by all of the coupon sources we list here, you will be happy to know that most of your coupon savings will come from these Sunday newspaper coupons. Just begin by focusing on those coupons and you can expand to other sources and strategies as you get the hang of using coupons.

The number and type of coupon offers in each newspaper's coupon circulars varies quite a bit. The two-hundred and fifty versions of SmartSource and Valassis coupon circulars are dependent on where advertisers want to place offers. For example, there are usually several newspapers within one state, and most likely the largest newspaper in the state will have the most coupon offers. Also, grocery products vary by region of the country, so coupons vary accordingly. Additionally, advertisers track their product's market-share by city, and thus may place more attractive offers (coupons with higher values) in markets where they want to increase their market-share. Finally, coupon values may even be coordinated with the local retailer's bonus coupon policies as manufacturers and retailers work together to attract shoppers.

I recognize that using and keeping track of coupons can be overwhelming—which is why most coupons go unused. The most positive feedback I get is from shoppers who had no success with coupons in the past but are now thrilled to share their stories of coupon savings. I do the work of finding the coupon deals and tell you where to find the coupon. Could it be any easier than that?

Internet Coupons

If you are a regular user of Sunday newspaper coupons, keep doing what you're doing. Discovering new sources of free coupons will help you save even more! When you view coupons as valuable currency, you'll begin to search for more sources of this free currency, including Internet coupons. There are two types of Internet coupons: printable Internet coupons, and targeted frequent shopper coupons.

Printable Internet Coupons

Found at specific websites, shoppers select the coupons they want and immediately print them on their home printers. At the time of this writing, most grocery stores accept these types of coupons, however some stores still won't due to coupon counterfeiting in 2003. Printable coupon sites have upgraded their security systems to prevent fraudulent activity, so we may see store policies relax over time. Be sure to ask your store about its policy regarding printable grocery coupons.

These coupons work exactly like newspaper coupons in terms of being doubled or tripled, based on your store's coupon bonus policy. The printable coupon sites listed here are easily found on the "Print Coupons" page on my website. You can also go directly to these sites: *CoolSavings.com, Boodle.com*, and *SmartSource.com*.

Targeted Frequent Shopper Coupons

Found on coupon websites, these offers are redeemable at a specific retailer. When the shopper selects the offers, the coupons are transferred electronically to the shopper's store discount card. The coupon value is deducted automatically at the register when the shopper buys the qualifying product. These coupons are deducted at face value and are not doubled. These Internet coupon technologies are promising in terms of ease to the shopper and affordability to the advertiser. Go to *Upons.com*.

Checkout Coupons

Offers generated from a coupon machine next to the register after you have completed your order are known as Catalina coupons (or electronic checkout coupons). The coupons are generated based on the products you purchased (for example, $1 off the competitor's brand of an item you purchased) or a cash coupon for a future order earned by purchasing qualifying items (for example, $1 off your next shopping order because you purchased the three items required). The system will automatically recognize qualifying items and generate the coupon. Because these offers may not be promoted or advertised, it pays to take a good look at your register-generated coupons.

Collecting Multiple Coupons

As I have discussed, the key to paying the lowest prices for grocery items at the store is to use grocery coupons when the item is on sale. The same companies featured in stores' sale flyers typically offer coupons for their products as well. They seek shoppers' attention in many ways, and may do it by offering several coupons in different resources at the same time, so it can be easy to collect multiple coupons for your favorite items.

Because stocking up on your key items when they are at their rock-bottom prices is key to saving big money, it is helpful to have more than one coupon for these key items on hand. Therefore learning how to collect multiple coupons for your key grocery items is critical to maximizing your grocery savings.

There are many creative, ethical ways to grow your coupon collection. However, buying and selling coupons is not one of them. This is illegal, and a disclaimer is printed on coupons specifying that they cannot be sold. (Go to *CouponInfo.com* for more information.)

Places to Find Coupons

1. *Sunday newspaper.* To get the most coupon offers in the circulars, look for the largest newspaper in your city or state. Look for special deals by calling the newspaper's sales office to ask about all of their promotional rates and compare them for the best deal. Another advantage to getting the paper delivered to your home is that you won't miss a week, so you won't miss great deals.

2. *Multiple newspapers.* Remember, they are recyclable. If you consider the return on your investment, you can see it makes sense. If you use $10 worth of coupons from each paper, they may be worth $15 after some of them are doubled at your store. With the average cost of a Sunday paper at $2, you are actually earning $13 with each additional paper you buy. If there are coupons for other stores you use (such as 40 percent off at your favorite craft store), the paper is worth even more.

If you check the Virtual Coupon Organizer on Sunday, you can quickly see which coupons are included in the paper that week and decide if it makes financial sense to buy extra copies. Some stores sell the Sunday paper at a discount after a certain time on Sundays.

3. *Soliciting extra copies for charity shopping.* Being a charity shopper is one of the best reasons to get extra copies of the coupon circular. If you are a regular coupon user and you use *CouponMom.com* to find the best

grocery deals at your store, you will easily see items marked with the word "charity" that are free, or almost free, every week. When these are items that your household doesn't use, it is extremely easy to buy them to contribute to charity since you are already cutting out coupons for your own shopping. If you had extra coupon circulars, you could buy more charity items and save more money on your own groceries.

You may be embarrassed to ask friends and neighbors for their coupon circulars for yourself, but soliciting friends and neighbors for their extra coupon circulars is easy when you are buying food for charity. You can make it easy for non-coupon-users to help the needy with little effort on their part by having a collection box for coupon circulars set up at your children's school, place of worship, workplace, exercise club, day-care center, or any other central location. Simply publicize the request, with an explanation of the charity-shopping concept, and watch the coupons come in. Be sure to explain that coupon circulars should not be cut out but turned in whole. This is even easier for coupon donors.

When I first began shopping for charity with coupons and asked neighbors for their coupon circulars, many faithfully dropped their coupons in my mailbox every week. After several weeks, I received a nice note from one neighbor, a busy working mother, thanking me for giving her this easy way to help others. When you use other people's coupon donations to buy more food for charity, be sure to let them know how much food you were able to buy and how many people their coupons helped feed. They will appreciate the opportunity to help in this way.

We have a coupon collection box at our children's school, and have found that children love to bring their coupon circulars in each week. And parents feel good about involving their children in helping others in this easy way. Shoppers who follow my Cut Out Hunger program use some of the coupons, and we give other coupon circulars to families in need to help them save on their groceries too.

A local church in my area also has a coupon collection box, which makes it easy for members to bring their circulars in on Sunday mornings. The coupons are given to a transitional housing program across the street to help their clients save money on groceries.

I'd like to share a story about one of my readers who figured out a way to help, even through her circumstances. Emily is a 79-year old woman who lives outside of Atlanta with her husband. She is homebound due to health reasons, but she realized after reading an article about me that she could help feed the hungry by cutting out coupons for charity shoppers. Emily sent me a large packet of perfectly cut coupons in care of my church. I wrote back thanking her, and included my home address. For over three years she has been faithfully sending me perfectly cut coupons. *In her first letter Emily wrote,*

> *"It seems to me that you could use these coupons to help oth-ers. I am not able to get out and volunteer anymore, but if you can use these then I know I can be of some help to those in need."*
>
> ~ *Emily, Georgia*

I always buy good deals for charity with some of Emily's coupons and share the rest with a family in need. She is indeed helping others and I tell her that every time.

4. *Manufacturer's websites.* If you have favorite brands of grocery items, send an email or letter to the manufacturer about how much you like their product(s). The majority of companies will in turn send coupons to their best customers if you include your mailing address. If you have a problem with a product, you should also contact them explaining your concern. The company may send you coupons to regain your goodwill.

5. *Sunday circulars.* Look for additional special coupon circulars in the

Sunday newspaper advertising section. You can expect to find Valassis and SmartSource coupon circulars each week, and some weeks you will find special circulars from individual manufacturers such as Procter & Gamble, Kraft, City of Hope (in Southern California), or from an individual grocery-store chain.

Typically coupon circulars are not published on holiday weekends such as Easter, Memorial Day, Labor Day, Fourth of July, Thanksgiving, and Christmas. However, you should always check my Virtual Coupon Organizer to see if new coupons are available that weekend so you don't miss a week.

6. *Product packaging.* There may be a coupon inside or outside of the box, or inside the label. I've purchased items with coupons placed inside the label that were higher in value than the item's sale price that week after the coupon was doubled—and I visited the store several times that week.

7. *Direct mail.* Retailers are investing quite a bit of money in direct-mail pieces, which will most likely include a valuable coupon to encourage you to shop at their store. Keep an eye out for mailings and check them for more coupons.

8. *Red-shelf boxes* (from the SmartSource company) are great sources for extra coupons. If the product featured is on sale, using the coupon on that visit makes sense. However, you may want to take an extra coupon or two for your coupon organizer, because the item's price may go even lower after the coupon box is taken down. These coupon boxes are changed every month and may vary by store, even stores in the same chain.

9. *In-store displays.* Many companies post tear-off pads of coupons on the shelf near their products or on the cardboard displays showcasing their products. Again, if the product is on sale it makes sense to use the coupon when you find it, but hold on to the coupon if the product is not

on sale and wait for its price to drop. You can also take extra coupons in case the product is on sale at a different store.

10. *Printable coupon sites.* Be sure to check all the sites since there may be a coupon offer for one of your items on more than one printable coupon site.

11. *Magazines.* Some magazines' grocery coupons are worth more than the cost of the magazine! If you use a coupon to buy the magazine, you will save even more. Woman's Day and Family Circle frequently issue coupons in the Sunday newspaper circulars to save when you buy single copies in the store. You can also get inexpensive annual subscriptions to popular magazines online at sites such as *NetMagazines.com* and *BestDealMagazines.com*.

12. *Rewards programs.* By joining rewards programs like *ClubMom.com* you'll automatically get a free subscription to Home Basics magazine, which includes many free grocery coupons.

13. *Store magazines.* Check with your store's customer-service counter for their specific information.

14. *Trade coupons.* If you have friends who use coupons, get together and share your lists of "coupon wants" with each other. For example, your friend with children in diapers would appreciate extra diaper coupons, and would happily trade coupons for your favorite items.

15. *Online coupon-trading group.* The Internet has become a gold mine of information for grocery and coupon information. Several websites provide message forums that allow members to share information about grocery deals in their stores as well as to connect with others to trade coupons by mail. Use a search engine for "grocery saving" or "coupon websites" to look for grocery deals and grocery coupon forums.

The Thrifty Fun website (*ThriftyFun.com*) has a message board called "the Coupon Swap." Here coupon users list the specific coupons they have to trade and those they want. Members trade coupons at no cost other than the postage to mail them. These sites are free to join, but you don't have to, and you can still view the messages and read the information (you will not be able to post replies or questions without joining the forum).

16. *Entertainment books.* In addition to having valuable coupons for many kinds of businesses and services, Entertainment books are filled with coupons for local grocery stores. Offers change slightly each year and vary by state, but it is worth checking. Go to *Entertainment.com* and preview your city's book. Call customer service to ask which grocery store coupons are available in your city's book. For example, in the 2005 book, shoppers in Texas could get a $5 off a $50 grocery-order coupon for two stores (Randall's and Kroger) each month! These coupons can also be used in combination with your typical manufacturers' grocery coupons. That means a Texas shopper who uses both stores could save as much as $10 per month, or $120 a year in groceries alone (the full price of the Entertainment book is $26). If you buy one from a local school or nonprofit organization, you also help the organization raise funds.

For a large family, it may make sense to buy more than one Entertainment book, particularly as the price of the book decreases over the course of the year (when you buy them from Entertainment's website). The new books come out in September each year and do not expire until the following November (fourteen months). I have seen the books go on sale for as low as $10 each with free shipping by the summer months, which still allows shoppers five to six months to use monthly grocery coupons.

17. *Manufacturers' email newsletters.* You will most likely be mailed free coupons or emailed free printable coupons for the products you prefer.

18. *In-store customer service.* In some cities, grocery stores place special advertising in newspapers that feature many grocery coupons. You may find coupons in the weekly store ad circular as well (both manufacturer's coupons and store coupons). Check the customer-service counter and pharmacy counter for brochures, flyers, and calendars that may include coupons.

19. *Grocery store websites.* The Pathmark grocery chain in the Northeast has an email newsletter that sends subscribers a one-cent coupon each week, which allows them to buy the specified item (worth about $1) for only one cent. Many chains are following suit. Weekly in-ad coupons are available from many stores, including Publix, Cub Foods, Ralphs, Vons, Safeway, and many others.

Nontraditional grocery-shopping options may offer printable coupons as well. For example, BJ's wholesale clubs (found in the Eastern part of the country) provide a selection of free printable coupons from their website, specific to their larger wholesale club sizes. For example, a recent week's selection of BJ's coupons included $1 off two ten-pound bags of name-brand flour, and $1.50 off a 35-count box of granola bars. Of course, you would need to be a member of BJ's wholesale club to take advantage of these coupons.

Super Target also has free printable coupons on their site for their own store's products. For example, one week's selection of grocery coupons on Super Target's site included coupons for fresh pineapple, fresh ground turkey, deli meat, and bakery cinnamon rolls, as well as more common coupons for cereal and yogurt. Because Super Target's coupons are labeled as store coupons, if you had a manufacturer's coupon from another source for the same item, you may be able to use them together. Keep in mind that Super Target stores do not double coupons.

20. *Newspaper websites.* Many newspapers have added a printable coupon option supplement with their Sunday coupon circulars.

As you can see, there is no shortage of free money available to you. Your potential coupon savings will grow dramatically when you are able to use the multiple-coupon strategy.

Now that you have all these resources—more than you'll ever need for your family—you can begin to feed your zip code too!

> *"The Coupon Mom showed me a better way of shopping. I heard about CouponMom.com and inquired. I have printed the coupons for myself, clipped from the papers and magazines and I have saved hundreds of dollars (really!). I have saved receipts to show others and share how coupons really work. I have encouraged others and just the other day at the day-care center when I picked up my kids I had an envelope with coupons in it for items I use. Someone even asked me if I had a particular coupon, and I did! It's been fun sharing the coupons and sharing our shopping stories. Right now on average I am saving 40 to 45 percent on my bill. It has been great!"*
>
> *~ Renee*

Chapter 9

How Strategic Shopping Benefits Others

In my early years of couponing I quickly came to realize that most people don't use coupons on a regular basis because of time and confusion. But I also came to realize that the benefits of couponing far outweighed the challenges, and not only for my family. As we began to see real savings, we became involved in a cause greater than ourselves.

It's difficult to imagine that hunger exists in the United States. We see the abundance of food everywhere we look. Even harder to understand is why people who are fully employed, and may work two or more jobs, are unable to afford to buy enough food for their families.

Before I became acquainted with a local charity in my area, I knew little about the reality of hunger and the challenges faced by those in need.

Did You Know?

Hunger is growing at its fastest rate among the working poor. When you consider that a full-time minimum-wage worker would earn $10,300 per year working forty hours per week, fifty weeks a year, it is no wonder that many households with a working adult cannot make ends meet. These days just the expenses of day care, housing, medical care, transportation, and food costs can easily exceed $10,300.

On a national average, extremely low incomes are defined as less than $13,590 for a family of four and $10,872 for a family of two[1]. Almost 70 percent of these households pay more than half of their income for housing, some housing that is severely inadequate. All too often, there isn't enough money left at the end of the month to adequately feed the children.

Many hardworking Americans struggle to meet their family's basic expenses. David Shiper, in his book *From The Working Poor: Invisible in America,* writes,

> *"The man who washes cars does not own one. The clerk who files cancelled checks at the bank has $2.02 in her own account. The woman who copy-edits medical textbooks has not been to a dentist in a decade.*
>
> *"This is the forgotten America. At the bottom of its working world, millions live in the shadow of prosperity, in the twilight between poverty and well-being. Whether you're rich, poor, or middle-class, you encounter them every day. They serve you Big Macs and help you find merchandise at Wal-Mart. They harvest your food, clean your offices, and sew your clothes[2]."*

I do not pretend to have solutions for the myriad of complex issues that contribute to poverty. I am simply a mother who saw an opportunity to help my community feed our neighbors. To help parents feed their children—at a very low cost. Over the five years of teaching my program, Cut Out Hunger, I've learned that plenty of people want to help their neighbors in this easy way.

I am thankful for our local charity's commitment to help my neighbors and am committed to helping them and charities like them meet the needs of their clients. I believe far more Americans can reach out where they live with Cut Out Hunger and make a difference in their neighbors' lives.

> *"Thank you so much for the service you provide. I am the Food Pantry Coordinator at Grace Rescue Mission in Phelan, California. I used to feel helpless that I could not do more for my clients beside the normal food bag we provide.*
>
> *"After using your website for about two months God has multiplied my blessings! I donate so much and can still stay way under my budget. My clients are now getting lots of extras like toothpaste and cleaning products. I have even found that I am able to sustain my family of five mostly on the coupon shopping I do once a week. Just as soon as I realize we need something, it turns up on sale! I am beginning a new program at our small, yet humble Mission.*
>
> *Your website will be a crucial part of our new program. And we'll be able to use the Virtual Coupon Organizer to find good deals at all the stores, even the ones not listed on your site."*
>
> ~ *Alicia, California*

Cut Out Hunger

I founded Cut Out Hunger to make it easy for the average shopper to buy food for charity with coupons. But I knew that the 10 percent of shoppers who use coupons regularly was not a large enough target market to fill our city's food pantries. To make a dent in local hunger, we needed to provide an easy way for all shoppers of all ages and all income levels to become potential food donors.

Over the past few years I have worked with non-coupon-users, children, teachers, and Georgia Tech college students to come up with creative solutions to make using coupons easy.

It was a full year and a half after I started Cut Out Hunger that I learned of similar couponing service websites in other states, but these sites charged for their information and didn't promote food donations.

Until then I hadn't even thought about charging for my information, because I was trying to attract shoppers to the idea of buying and donating food for charity. By that time I had seen such tremendous growth and positive response to my Cut Out Hunger program that I knew charging a fee, even a small one, would limit its growth unnecessarily. My solution to defray expenses was to add appropriate advertising to the site so I will never have to charge a fee.

This is the basic concept of "teaching a man to fish." We can give a man fish to eat today, or we can teach a man to fish so he can feed himself for the rest of his life. I have personally worked with shoppers in financial crisis and have experienced great satisfaction watching them learn how to cut their grocery bills dramatically. They not only save money but their confidence increases as they become more self-sufficient. They have also taught friends and neighbors how to use the system. Because of the potential of this program to help shoppers, be assured that I will never charge a fee to use my website.

CutOutHunger.org began as a hobby, and I maintained it in my spare time (my real job was being a mother to two young boys). I certainly did not have the luxury of an advertising budget, a public relations director, a corporate sponsor, or data-entry staff.

I was passionate about the concept, had seen it work, knew it had potential, but I felt overwhelmed with the seemingly impossible task of "marketing" the website. However, I couldn't imagine abandoning the concept because of its obvious potential. After the initial round of news coverage in its first year, the site leveled off to a user base of a thousand people a month. With over four million grocery shoppers in Georgia alone, it hadn't even come close to its potential.

When I shared my challenge with a friend who worked with a successful charity, she suggested that I start small, focus on my neighborhood, and "tackle my zip code." If we saw a noticeable change in our charity's donations, and if other people took ownership of the concept and helped spread the word, we could use what we had learned in our zip code and share it with other cities.

That seemed manageable to me, so I took her advice. Few of us are likely to change the world, but each of us is able to make a difference in our own zip code. I didn't need advertising or funding if I simply communicated the program in my own sphere of influence, for example area schools, places of worship, neighborhoods, civic organizations, youth groups, and scouts.

It worked. In fact, so many people and organizations in my community took ownership of the concept that even more great ideas were added to the program. I have shared some of those ideas on the website, and thousands of people in other cities have implemented them in their own zip codes. Many people in other cities have also suggested new ideas that I've put on the website, multiplying the benefit of their ideas with thousands of other Cut Out Hunger shoppers across the country.

Each of us is capable of making a difference where we live, regardless of our income level or age. If enough of us "tackle our zip codes," together we will make a major difference in the lives of millions of people in need all over our country.

Beyond the Annual Food Drive

To learn more about the reality of hunger in our country as a whole and in your own state specifically, I encourage you to visit the Second Harvest website, *SecondHarvest.org*. It is our country's largest hunger organization and their site provides detailed and interesting research findings as well as actual client stories regarding this complex issue.

Second Harvest manages a network of two hundred central food banks, which provide more than two billion pounds of food to those in need via local community food pantries that get much of their food from central food banks. However, local food pantries must also rely on local food donations and food drives to meet their clients' needs.

Americans tend to donate the most food to charity during local food drives. Makes sense. But the majority of large food drives are held during the winter holiday season, typically beginning with Thanksgiving. It is great that Americans respond generously during the holiday season, and I hope that more people will donate to annual food drives by using the Cut Out Hunger system. However, charities need our donations all year long because people are in need all year long. We need to donate food on a year-round basis if we hope to fill the shortages in our food pantries.

The generosity of Americans and passionate volunteerism has created this local "safety net" of food pantries and charities all over the country, but charities struggle with a lack of awareness. In addition, many potential food donors have no idea where the nearest charity is located or that the charity may need to ration food supplies in order to serve their clients. Far more of us could easily support our own local charities if we became more familiar with them.

Donating one item a week is all it takes to make a difference in the fight against hunger. Simple math supports this concept. In my suburb at least ten thousand shoppers go through my local grocery store in a week. There are at least five major grocery stores within a five-mile radius of our suburb's food pantry. I know our high-volume charity sees a hundred families a day, distributing ten thousand items per week. If every shopper in my suburb donated one item per weekly shopping trip, that would add up to fifty thousand donated items per week. It would only take 20 percent of shoppers buying one item a week to generously supply the food pantry.

Let's assume we are each part of that 20 percent. Let's set the example for our children to give at least one item per week as a habit so they will carry that mentality into the next generation.

Cut Out Hunger While You Shop

Even if you think you can't afford to donate food to charity, I can show you how to buy good charity items every week for only pennies. Buying as few as one or two items a week for charity may not seem significant in the fight against hunger, but it becomes a very significant contribution over the course of a year. Donating fifty to a hundred good food items a year to charity is far more than the average American donates to charity, and a Cut Out Hunger shopper can do that for mere pennies a week (or even get items free with a coupon).

The Cut Out Hunger system is also an efficient way to help others. Many parents of young children tell me that it's difficult to volunteer outside of the home. Incorporating the Cut Out Hunger approach in their regular shopping routine not only saves them money but also provides them an easy way to give and teaches their children that helping others is an important part of daily life.

In addition to being an efficient and inexpensive system, Cut Out Hunger introduces a new way of giving that is extremely rewarding. Period. I cannot adequately describe the wonderful experience of personally donating a box of food—you just have to try it yourself. You will probably become a regular food donor once you have handed your food to a grateful volunteer; heard a food-pantry client say, "Thank you—you are doing a good thing for us"; watched the smile on your child's face when the food-pantry volunteer thanks him for his generosity; or heard your child say, "Mom, it makes me sad to see the people at the food pantry, but I always feel better when we take food for them."

I have heard from many people across the country who implement Cut Out Hunger in their communities. This is the most exciting part of this project, and I am immensely thankful for the generous and compassionate people who are responding to this need.

"I saw a local TV news story with you shopping and racking up astounding grocery savings. I was pretty excited after seeing that news story, so I started using your site and have seen a substantial reduction in our budget for food and household items.

"While the savings have been wonderful, I was not donating any food to help the hungry prior to seeing the story, but I am now. I'm starting small, just trying to add $2 to $3 to my weekly grocery bill for items I want to donate. This amounts to $10 per month, but used in conjunction with your site, that $10 goes further than I would have ever imagined, filling a whole box in October and already most of a box in November.

"When I started doing this, I was excited for the weekly savings at the grocery store. Now I'm more excited about how much food I can donate for $3. The financial savings are becoming secondary.

"Prior to finding your site, I never really gave much thought about trying to help hungry and needy families in Denver. Now it is something that is on my mind every single week."

~ Jeffrey, Colorado

Chapter 10

How to Cut Out Hunger
Where You Live

One of my favorite stories is about Jeff, a businessman I met while on an airplane from Denver to Atlanta as we both returned from family ski trips. His family's seating arrangements were mixed up, so he got stuck for three hours in the middle seat next to the Coupon Mom. Can you imagine?

I can't remember how long I spent telling him about Cut Out Hunger, probably just two hours and forty-five minutes, but he remembered. He seemed interested in learning how to start the concept in his Atlanta suburb. He asked for the website address and contact information. I thought he was only being polite.

A few weeks later I received a call from Jeff. He had met with the leadership group at his church and explained the Cut Out Hunger concept. The group decided to work with the local food pantry and the nearby grocery store to publicize the food pantry's need, to put a year-round collection bin in the store for donations, and to arrange to have the food picked up from the store by food-pantry volunteers.

Jeff had written a detailed plan. He coordinated meetings with others who shared his interest and began to publicize the program within his church, at his children's school, and in the community. Jeff updates me periodically to let me know that they are donating more food to the local charity and the director is very appreciative of their efforts. Last time Jeff called me to report their progress, I asked, "Is there anything you need me to do?" Jeff said, "No, I just wanted to let you know what we are doing." That's my kind of program!

Jeff took the concept and applied it in his sphere of influence, in much the same way he approached gaining cooperation in his career and other volunteer programs. I have similar accounts from mothers who have taught their Girl Scout troops how to buy food for charity, men who have taught grocery-saving seminars in their workplaces, and women who have taught similar seminars to their women's groups. Each one of us has our own way of approaching others to gain cooperation, and we can make a difference in our own spheres of influence.

Get Started!

1. *Get to know the needs of your local food pantry.* If you do not know where your nearest food pantry is located, you can find that information on the Second Harvest website (*SecondHarvest.org*). As I've mentioned, food banks are large central organizations that warehouse food for charity (donated primarily from food manufacturers and grocery chains) and distribute it to smaller community hunger organizations, which in turn distribute the food directly to clients—people in need. Your city's food bank should be able to identify the food pantry in your immediate community.

Go to the local food pantry and speak with the director or a volunteer to learn more about the people they serve, what they distribute, and what the charity needs. It is much easier to respond to the needs in our community when we understand exactly what they are and connect personally with the people on the front lines of the issue. When we meet a hard-working, compassionate food-pantry volunteer who has to turn families in need away because they don't have enough food, we get motivated to help. Personally connecting with your local charity will make starting to "cut out hunger" easier.

2. *Work with your local grocery store manager to have a year-round collection bin in the store for your local charity.* Collection bins in the grocery stores are the key to helping shoppers donate food conveniently. Shoppers are much more likely to buy an extra item every week if they have a convenient place to donate it. This simple idea can help feed hundreds of people each year.

Unfortunately it is not easy to get year-round collection bins in every grocery store in a city through the grocery-store's headquarters. The central coordination and management of that process is labor-intensive, time-consuming, and expensive. That's why most grocery stores focus their food-drive efforts on one annual food drive that benefits one central hunger organization.

However, the grocery store is the obvious place to collect food on a year-round basis—it is where we buy food, and thousands of shoppers walk its aisles each week.

When we work with local stores individually, we have found it easier to set up a food-donation collection bin in our own stores year-round. The manager will need a community volunteer to empty the bin and deliver it to the food pantry (I do it for my store). The store manager may have a large collection bin to use, or can make one from a large box. The volunteer should offer to make a sign for the bin indicating what it is and the name of the benefiting charity. The local food pantry also may be able to arrange to have the food picked up as needed. Initially it can take a full month for a large collection bin to fill in a store, but once the concept catches on, it may fill every week.

If you approach your store manager with this concept and sense any reluctance on his part, simply promise to assume responsibility for making sure the bin is emptied regularly and the food goes to a reputable food pantry (the store will need to approve your selected food pantry). Be sure the manager knows that you will be working to raise awareness in the community about the bin at his store—it can actually increase customer traffic to the store. Store managers are generally happy with a program that encourages shoppers to buy more food at their stores!

3. *Promote the idea of donating "one item per week."* Whenever I speak to youth groups, women's groups, civic groups, or school classes, I always emphasize that if every American bought one item per week for charity, we would literally flood our local food pantries and enable them to do a much better job feeding families in need. When we consider that the average family spends $100 to $200 per week on their own groceries, and that it is possible to buy good items (without even having coupons) for 33 cents per week, donating food is a realistic and affordable habit. Most weeks there are items that are free with a coupon, but shoppers do not have to use coupons if they don't want to—they can simply look for store-brand items on sale that are appropriate for charity.

Our grocery-store manager allowed us to set up a special table of potential "charity items" in the store that we stocked from their shelves, with sale items such as peanut butter, tuna, rice, canned vegetables, and so on. We promoted the "one item a week" idea at our school, and parents told me they enjoyed having their children select the charity items each week from the table and donate them to the collection bin. The collection bin overflowed and had to be emptied every week that summer. The grocery-store manager even noticed a dramatic increase in their tuna sales!

4. *Help individuals in need with food donations.* When our neighborhood learned that our children's bus driver had a family medical and financial crisis that led to her family's electricity being turned off in the winter, we quickly coordinated efforts to help her family financially, as well as with food donations we purchased using coupons. She had been a caring and conscientious bus driver for our neighborhood for fifteen years. We were distraught and shocked to learn that her family had been suffering and we hadn't known. We got the word out, and soon money, clothes, toys, and food poured in for her family.

Although her situation was traumatic, it gave us the opportunity to show her how important she was to us, and how much we appreciated her kindness toward our children. I taught her how to use my website to cut her family's grocery bill, and we now have a collection box at our school for coupon circulars that we give to her, which helps her save far more money on groceries. She in turn taught her neighbors how to use the site and shares coupons with them.

I have received many stories from people telling how they were able to help friends, neighbors, and family members with food donations. They have told me that their loved ones are also more willing to accept food donations (especially when they know you bought them for a very low price) than money. It's an easy way to show both financial and moral support to help people through difficult times.

5. *Teach others how to use the Cut Out Hunger program to save money on groceries.* Many Cut Out Hunger shoppers use the website as a teaching tool for workshops and seminars to teach groups how to save money. Most Americans are interested in easy ways to save money. This program can give you an easy way to engage others in the idea of saving money and using grocery coupons, which naturally leads to donating items to charity at a very low cost.

6. *Promote the Cut Out Hunger program to other influencers.* When we began promoting in our zip code, we began by asking our local places of worship, schools, grocery stores, and food pantries to include articles about Cut Out Hunger in their newsletters, to post links on their websites, and to put flyers on bulletin boards. Parents at our school took the idea to other places of worship, scout groups, and other schools. We met with and gained support from regional presidents of organizations like PTA (Parent/Teachers Association), Kiwanis Clubs, Rotary Clubs, Girl Scouts; other food pantry directors; the school district's communications department; Consumer Credit Counseling Service of Atlanta; and Georgia's Department of Labor (to help unemployed workers save money on groceries). The Cut Out Hunger concept spread to other schools and communities across Georgia as a result of their influence.

7. *Reach out to the local media.* I have learned that the media does the best job of spreading the word on Cut Out Hunger. In fact, news stories are responsible for reaching almost all of my site users, in my own zip code and across the country.

I'd like to introduce you to Joe Jackson. He is a 44-year-old husband and father of four who lives in the Atlanta area. Joe has always been a bargain shopper, but when he read an article about Cut Out Hunger in the newspaper he began to buy food for charity. Two years later in June of 2003 the same newspaper ran a feature story on Joe and his efforts to feed the hungry. The journalist wrote of Joe's grocery couponing skills,

> *"It's a skill the father learned from his father. It became an art when Joe himself fell on hard times and needed to feed his family of six. He started slowly. But then a couple of years ago he discovered a website that turned his art into major savings and an opportunity to give to others. Said Joe of* CouponMom.com, *'It opened my eyes to all the free items that I could get.'"*

Joe donated over $300 in groceries to his local food pantry. The president of the charity said,

> *"If people like Joe didn't bring food to us, we'd have to barter and beg. He's a real blessing."*

Joe has taught seminars at his church and in his community and has helped many people learn how to cut out hunger in their community.

The Cut Out Hunger concept has been tested and reported by dozens of newspapers, radio stations, and television stations across the country. The idea of saving so much money at the grocery store is popular with just about everyone, and hunger is a unifying cause about which most Americans care deeply.

If you are willing to demonstrate or share the program with your local media, they will probably be interested in reporting on your activities to help raise awareness with their viewers, listeners, or readers. Several Cut Out Hunger shoppers across the country have taken reporters on shopping trips to demonstrate the program where they live, and as a result, have helped gain countless food donors in their own communities.

If you are interested in raising support to end hunger in your community, simply email or call the news contacts in your area and see if they are interested in seeing a demonstration of the Cut Out Hunger savings and donation program. You can also contact your local media outlets to report on specific outreach efforts of your club or organization, or a specific food-donation event you have organized.

Examples of Compassion

I am in awe of the many creative ways people have used Cut Out Hunger in their zip codes. Hundreds of people tell me about the satisfaction they've received by raising food donations for charities in their zip codes. Here are a couple of their stories:

"When I approached the youth leader at a local church about the idea of involving their vacation Bible school students in the Cut Out Hunger program, she was immediately interested.

"Every summer this parish holds a one-week vacation Bible school attended by hundreds of young children. The youth group leader thought of a new idea: to hold a contest to see which age group could bring in the most money in the form of spare change they received from their parents, which they then would use to buy food for charity by the case. Each day hundreds of children brought in pennies, nickels, dimes, and quarters to add to the collection.

"After a week, the kids had collected $1,526 in cash. They purchased dozens of cases of nutritious food items for the charity by using my website, and fed hundreds of people with very little effort. I couldn't believe the amount of money they raised, so I asked our local newspaper to write an article about it and take a picture of the children. Their article showed the winning age group, several four-year-old children sitting on the cases of food they had purchased.

"If four-year-olds can feed the hungry this easily, imagine the potential we have if youth groups of all ages were to raise public awareness of the ease of helping others."

~ St. Brigid Catholic Church, Alpharetta, Georgia

One of the earliest supporters of Cut out Hunger was Mt. Pisgah Methodist Church, a large church in the Atlanta area. They were already active supporters of the local charity and had learned about my plan from our food-pantry director.

They publicized the website address to their six thousand members, held training workshops on how to use the program, and had their youth group hold Cut out Hunger food drives in their grocery store. They worked with a local grocery-store manager to arrange for a collection bin in that store on a year-round basis, and their church volunteers pick up and deliver the food to the local food pantry.

Church members incorporate the Kids Cut Out Hunger program (you will learn about this in the next chapter) in their church youth groups and with classes in their elementary schools. Church members promote the program within their schools and PTA-sponsored community outreach committees. Mt. Pisgah's approach is a perfect example of how easily the concept of regular food donations can be implemented in our daily routines if we make it easy for shoppers to donate and incorporate programs in our organizations and schools.

I also have heard from several young mothers' groups who have used the program to raise large amounts of food for charity by organizing their efforts. The members all bring in their Sunday coupons, a few members are designated as "shoppers," and each member donates a dollar or two each to pay for the groceries. A mothers' group in Marietta, Georgia, reported donating twenty-five bags of groceries worth $381 for only $98. Another mothers' group in Ft. Worth, Texas, donated 321 items worth $332 for a total cost of only $28. Some groups make it an annual project, others monthly.

I've heard stories from Cut Out Hunger shoppers who have organized efforts within their communities and places of worship to collect grocery coupons and use the Best-Deals List at *CutOutHunger.org* to buy items for soldiers stationed overseas, sending large packages of supplies at a very low cost. A church in Atlanta shared their story of organizing supplies for hurricane victims.

One of my favorite stories came from a college student in California. She read about Cut Out Hunger in a magazine article, and contacted me to learn about how she could teach this concept to children for her final school project. We spoke by phone and email, and she later reported that she successfully taught ninety sixth graders how to buy food for charity with coupons. They donated hundreds of items to their local food pantry and she got an A.

Cut Out Hunger has taught me that Americans truly care about helping others, and they appreciate learning new, easy ways to do so. I have also discovered countless creative applications for the program to help others, and I am thrilled to add new ideas to the program as they evolve. I want to hear from you. Please share your stories by emailing me via *CouponMom.com*. I love to read about your successes and experiences and share them with others.

"On behalf of North Fulton Community Charities, I congratulate you on the publishing of your book that will help others put Cut Out Hunger into practice. There are many programs that offer tips on saving money but Cut Out Hunger incorporates the importance of reaching out to help someone else at the same time.

"We first met when you were delivering donated food items from your church to the Food Pantry. Our food supplies were depleted and the food you brought was quickly put in bags for the many families who came for food assistance. I remember the concern in your eyes. People didn't have enough food. How could people be going hungry in an area of metro Atlanta known for comfortable living? We talked about the fact that many people don't know what kind of food makes the best gift to a Food Pantry. We laughed over the cans of artichokes and olives on the Pantry shelf. Our conversation started you thinking about how you could help.

"At first you and a few friends tested the idea of using coupons to save money for personal shopping and to purchase needed items for charity. You compiled lists and spreadsheets of Two-for-One sales and store specials. As word of your ability to shop and save money spread, food started arriving in our Food Pantry by the grocery-cart full. Cut Out Hunger shoppers would say, "You won't believe how much I saved this week and still bought all this food for the Pantry." People who had never donated food before, other than a can or two when the children's school had a food drive, began to make it part of their budget to buy food for charity.

"You have taken a simple idea and with unflagging energy and determination created a new way of shopping. You have continued to emphasize the importance of filling local Food Pantry shelves with basic food that people need. I am especially delighted to see that often the shoppers are children who are learning positive values."

~ Barbara S. Duffy, Executive Director

Chapter 11

Get Kids Involved

By the second year of Cut Out Hunger, we wanted to involve children in buying food for charity. After all, it is possible to buy food with coupons for only pennies, so we figured children could afford it too. Also, when we teach children how to give to charity at a young age, they are more likely to develop a lifelong habit of giving.

I wasn't sure exactly how to go about teaching children how to shop with grocery coupons, so I asked my oldest son's third-grade teacher for ideas. She invited me to her classroom to teach the children how to make grocery lists and cut out coupons as part of a math lesson.

The concept made sense and helped the class practice their math and money skills. However, the teacher immediately recognized that the process of cutting out and organizing coupons every week was cumbersome, so we needed an easier way for children to manage coupon organization.

That twenty-two-year-old teacher's idea was one of the most important improvements to the Cut Out Hunger program to date. Her suggestion was to have the children write the date on the front of the two coupon circulars each week. She asked me to add the date when the coupon came out next to each "deal" listed on my website each week. This way, when the children saw the three or four items they planned to buy, they only needed to look in that particular circular and cut out the few coupons they needed. Brilliant! It was much easier than having them cut out more than a hundred coupons every week when they used only a few. That suggestion became a new feature on the website for all users, including adults, and has made it much easier for many people to use coupons.

Additionally, this teacher suggested that we list grocery items that were appropriate for charities and did not require coupons. This would make it easier for children to participate if parents didn't want to use coupons at all. That suggestion made sense. For example, tuna is one of the most important charity-donation items. A typical sale price for store-brand tuna is 33 cents a can—certainly manageable on an eight-year-old's budget!

Another suggestion was to give children a suggested shopping budget in terms they could understand. For example, our school has a monthly roller-skating party that many children attend after school. It costs $3.50 for admission. She suggested children create shopping lists by selecting items from the website's Best-Deals List that add up to $3.50. Not only was this a good math exercise but it showed them how many people could be helped for a relatively small amount of money.

Finally, she asked me to arrange an after-school field trip to the grocery store for the children to buy groceries for charity with their lists. This was easy to do. The grocery management included a fun tour for the students, and the children received their own store discount cards, which they thought was great. Some of the children even asked their neighbors to donate unused coupon circulars so they would be able to buy more food for charity. When all the children had bought their groceries, saving an average of 70 percent, they put them in one shopping cart overflowing with their purchases.

I was so thrilled with their success that I called the Atlanta Journal-Constitution newspaper, which in turn published an article on February 14, 2002, about the children's efforts. The newspaper took pictures of the students cutting out coupons in class and interviewed them about the project. They were able to buy 122 items, enough to provide eight families with a supply of food at the food pantry. One third-grade boy said, "We saved so much we were all jumping with joy. We saved $83."

The idea was a winner, so we taught several school classes how to buy food for charity and then arranged shopping field trips for them that year. We asked the store to keep a food-collection bin in the store on a year-round basis, and parents began buying food for charity with their children. To this day, the bin fills up every single month and has for four years.

We added a section to my website called "Kids Program" and provided instructions on how to organize group field trips at a grocery store based on our experience. You can even see a picture of the first group of students who tested the Kids Program!

A Fifteen-Year-Old's Creative Genius

One of the most ingenious ideas I've heard that helps all parties involved is what Dana Tanner of Roswell, Georgia, does each week with her son's help.

Dana's fifteen-year-old son needed to earn his own spending money, and Dana wanted to save money on her family's groceries. She didn't have the time to use coupons, and her son's busy academic and extracurricular schedule made it difficult for him to work at a job during the school year. Therefore she taught him how to use the Cut Out Hunger site to plan their family's grocery lists, using coupons. He cuts out and organizes the coupons to match the list, making it easy for Dana to shop efficiently and save dramatically. Each week Dana notes the savings number at the bottom of the store receipt. She gives a third of the savings to her son and he then selects a favorite charity and donates another third to them. For example, recently she gave a third of the $36 weekly savings to her son ($12, not a bad allowance) and he selected a local charity to receive another $12 of their savings that week. Week by week the savings—and thus his earnings and the charity's donations—grow. Dana benefits by keeping the remaining third. Their family saves money and earns money, and they also help the less fortunate in the community. Not only that, but her son is learning valuable savings skills that will help him financially throughout his life.

Teaching Kids How to Shop

As parents and teachers, it is not difficult to make a positive impression with children when it comes to creatively helping others in need. They soak up new ideas like sponges; they do not suffer from being cynical; and they feel wonderful when they accomplish new skills.

I received a great letter from one of my readers sharing her experience with her daughter's Girl Scout troop. Colleen is a mother of three and she thought it would be a fun way to teach her daughter's Girl Scout troop about feeding the hungry and stretching their dollars at the same time. Colleen took a group of nine-year old girls on a shopping trip to the local grocery store. The girls used *CouponMom.com* to plan their shopping lists, organize their coupons and find the best deals for charity. They filled a shopping cart with food for charity and saved over 60 percent on their bill. The activity helped them earn their Hunger patch, and prompted the idea of my working with the Girl Scout Council of Atlanta.

Shopping is an adult activity that children are used to watching, but not doing and they generally have little to do with the charitable contributions their families make each year. But kids want to be involved in what adults are doing. The Kids Cut Out Hunger program allows them to help others in a hands-on, direct way. Teaching our children how to be givers has long-term benefits for both our children and those they help.

One day a soft-spoken nine-year-old girl at my sons' school brought a large bag of groceries that she had purchased for charity. She was excited about what she had done and happy to report her Cut Out Hunger success to our school's office manager. The child's face lit up as she confidently explained how she had purchased many groceries with coupons and a little money. I read this article that she wrote in the school newsletter and couldn't help but get choked up.

> *"I learned from Mrs. Nelson that there is so much food we can buy to help others. She taught us how to "Cut Out Hunger" by using coupons to save money and to donate food items to the hungry. I bought food for $1 and less! I bought three chocolate pies, which were free with a coupon. I also bought macaroni and cheese for 39 cents and tomato sauce for 40 cents.*
>
> *"I bought cereal bars on sale for $1 and with another coupon paid only 75 cents. I bought beans with bacon for 50 cents. There are so many items you can buy for only $1 or less. So if I could do all that, then you could do it too. You can cut out hunger just like me!"*
>
> ~ *Jasleen, 9 years old*

The Charity Sale Table Concept Is Born

In the program's second year, I was teaching my son's fourth-grade class how to use the Cut Out Hunger program to prepare them for their store field trip. Their teacher had led an effort for years to help a local charity by raising donations at the school. Her students were familiar with the food needs in our local community because they had visited the food pantry as a group. They were excited to learn how to help in a new way. The teacher had always solicited ideas from the children (the idea to help support the charity had come from a student years before), and this day was no exception. As I ended my presentation, the teacher asked the students if they had any ideas for me.

One girl raised her hand and said, "Mrs. Nelson, what if we had a lemonade stand in the grocery store and we asked shoppers to buy food for charity? We could hand out free lemonade to shoppers who bought food."

Interesting. I had never thought of that idea. I looked at the teacher, who smiled and said, "Mrs. Nelson, would you be willing to set that up with the grocery-store manager for next Wednesday after school?" Any mother knows you do not say no to a teacher!

I called the store manager and asked if we could set up a lemonade stand for charity in his store and he responded, "Of course you can. We should never discourage initiative in children."

The following Wednesday several students met at the grocery store. We stocked a card table at the store entrance with good "charity deals" that did not require coupons and then made a simple sign and price tags for the items displayed. As shoppers walked by, the children asked them if they would be willing to buy a few items with their shopping order for the local charity. Shoppers took the items, and after their purchase the students stood by the collection bin at the exit door thanking them and handing out free cookies and lemonade to the generous shoppers.

Shoppers responded positively—after all, the items only cost 33 cents, took little effort to purchase, and the students knowledgeably described the charity that needed the food. The children had visited the charity. They knew why people needed food and wanted to help. As a result, many shoppers purchased charity items from the children's display table to donate to the collection bin.

The children's idea worked. In only two hours after school, a handful of ten-year-old children collected six hundred items from shoppers—enough to help forty families in need.

I was beside myself with excitement. This idea was fabulous—charity sale tables. Imagine how much food would be donated to charity if hundreds of school groups, scout groups, and church youth groups held such an event only once a year! I went to work spreading the word about this ten-year-old girl's idea to local churches, other schools, Kiwanis clubs, and scout leaders. In that first year dozens of youth organizations in my suburb held charity sale tables and continue this project on an annual basis.

One Cub Scout pack in Marietta, Georgia, holds the record for the highest number of items sold in one day—three thousand items for charity sold on one Saturday. Each scout, along with one parent, volunteered for a two-hour shift. They provided food for two hundred families.

Children Shopping with Parents (One Item Per Week)

Although many groups have raised a high volume of food donations with the Kids Cut Out Hunger program, I believe its greatest potential to raise food donations long-term is by having parents individually work with their children to shop for charity on a regular basis.

I have received stories from young mothers who involve their children as young as two or three years old in selecting "one item per week" for charity. The children may even hold the coupon for their one item and help buy the item at the register. It is an easy way for a busy mother to incorporate a good lesson into her regular routine. I've had mothers tell me that when they have forgotten to buy the charity item, their children have reminded them.

I know my nine- and twelve-year-old sons enjoy having their own shopping list for charity, finding the items, carrying their basket, and buying the items at the register. I believe it helps them learn valuable money and budgeting skills, and it helps them keep the idea of helping others in mind all year long, not just during the holiday season.

We keep a box in our garage for charity items. Each week we put our charity purchases in that box, and we make a delivery to our food pantry about once a month. My children do not always like to go to the food pantry because it makes them sad, but they tell me they always feel better after we have donated the food. I tell them I understand how they feel—it makes me sad too. If it didn't, I don't know if we'd be donating food. I believe they call that sadness compassion, and we need it to motivate us to help.

Having compassion leads to helping others, and helping others leads to indescribable joy. Encourage children to experience this at a young age and there is a good chance they will continue the habit throughout life. They will teach it to their children, and so on, and so on, and so on.

To date, hundreds of kids have participated in a charity-sale-table activity as part of a youth service project sponsored by their place of worship, school, scout troop or youth group. In every instance they have been able to raise large quantities of much-needed items for charity in a short amount of time, with relatively little organization required.

Parents appreciate being able to involve their kids in community-service activities where they live. Children gain confidence as shoppers respond positively to their efforts and those efforts result in hundreds of food donations. I love hearing a child tell me, "It makes me happy to help feed the hungry, I want to do this again!"

"Mrs. Nelson, one of my student's moms, shared with my class how to use coupons to help the hungry. Her presentation was age-appropriate and she brought in a load of coupons for all the kids to cut out, sharing which ones featured food that was healthier than others. The kids had a field day cutting out coupons like adults do! She then went through the process of explaining how to save, organize, and use the coupons in conjunction with her website on a weekly basis. However, I was having a difficult time organizing all of this information in my head, and assumed my eight- and nine-year olds were too. But Mrs. Nelson and I devised a simplified version for kids to use.

"The Cut Out Hunger program at CouponMom.com now features that 'kids' list,' which highlights foods to purchase for the hungry. It is a condensed version, which allows a child to check out the list and know exactly what to look for. We even took into account that not every household saves their coupons; that even with the influence of Mrs. Nelson in their lives, the kids had no control over the Sunday paper.

"I got to thinking how much my students enjoyed Mrs. Nelson's program and the value of teaching kids to give back and help out. I remembered in my first year teaching, I tried to attend the school's monthly skating parties. I would encourage the kids to attend, too, and we won the 'Golden Skate' award numerous times. Admission for the parties cost each child $3.50. With that memory came another idea for Kids Cut Out Hunger!

"If students were willing to go to a skating party, wouldn't they

also be interested in going to the grocery store with their friends and teachers? Absolutely! I decided to give it a try. We created shopping lists, sticking with our skating party admission budget of $3.50.

"The grocery store filled with happy children, ready parents, and a hopeful teacher. We had a tour, which included decorating cookies, touching a LIVE lobster, and actually shopping. The results were unbelievable! Fifteen students purchased items all on their own that later went to our local food bank. Talk about a sense of ownership for the kids. Eight- and nine-year olds were helping to feed the hungry! Not only did it teach the students an incredibly valuable lesson, it also made an amazing impression on the parents who attended.

"As the program at our school evolved, we set up various shopping trips and charity sale tables. Students felt empowered by how many people they could influence to purchase charity sale items. They saw the collection bin fill past the brim and the sound of their laughter was magical.

"Over the past four years, from coupon cutting marathons to shopping adventures, the school has created an even larger avenue to Cut Out Hunger. We have established a Community Outreach Committee involving our students and parents. We call it the HOWL committee…Helping Others With Love. We originally began with the idea that our group would benefit Cut Out Hunger and a local homeless shelter, but as the word got out about what we were doing, additional organizations that we helped just continued to fall in our laps. Every year, the students are trained in how to use the Cut Out Hunger website to build a shopping list for the hungry. We organize off-campus meetings at the local grocery store to put our work into action. We do skits to allow the members to gain awareness and training on how to run a Charity Sale Table. The most exciting thing about the Cut Out

Hunger program, is the fact that on random days, food items will show up on my desk, a book of coupons will just be lying there...the students, anywhere from eight to eleven, feel like they can help. And when a person at that age knows empathy...imagine what will they do to Help Others With Love for the rest of their lives?"

~ Stephanie Meyer, 3rd grade teacher, Georgia

136

Chapter 12

Helping Others One Zip Code at a Time

With the popularity of my Cut Out Hunger program among kids, I decided it was time to brainstorm age-appropriate ways kids of all ages could become involved. Leave it to kids to energize adults and enlist their help in something as worthwhile as ending hunger in America!

Getting children and youth groups involved in the Kids Cut Out Hunger program has spread like wildfire across the country. I hope it will be helpful to share some of the projects that have proven effective.

Youth Service Projects

Middle-School Youth Group Projects

Many youth groups require community service hours to complete their programs. A confirmation class at a local Catholic church in my area organizes a charity sale table one Saturday a month at five area grocery stores. Children raise hundreds of items every month to help stock the church's food pantry that serves those in need.

Cub Scout "Scouting for Food" Projects

Many scouting groups across the country raise food for charity as part of their community-service programs. Cub Scouts in the Atlanta area have raised thousands of food items by designating one day a year as "Cut Out Hunger" day, staffing a few area grocery stores with scouts at charity sale tables for a full day (Saturday, from 9 A.M. to 5 P.M.). Each scout and his parent staffs a two-hour shift, and scout leaders make arrangements with the grocery-store managers to preorder cases of appropriate food items for charity. Many shoppers voluntarily donate money for the food pantry as well. Cub Scout packs in our Atlanta suburb have held these events three years in a row, and have increased their results each year.

Vacation Bible School Outreach Projects

During the summer, many churches across the country hold one-week vacation Bible schools. Some churches use the charity sale table as their community service project for the week, staffing a few area stores for one morning. Again, they successfully raise hundreds of food items for the local food pantry. Summertime is the most difficult time of the year to collect food-pantry supplies, as there are few food drives, so this is an excellent way to make a difference and teach children a valuable lesson.

School Community-Outreach Club Projects

Many middle schools, high schools and some elementary schools sponsor Community Outreach Clubs for their students. The charity sale table has successfully been used by clubs of all ages, and afterward students wanted to do it again. The time spent staffing the tables, preparing and organizing the event, and delivering the food to the charity also qualifies as community-service credit for older students needing to fulfill those requirements.

How to Organize a Charity Sale Table

1. *Contact the manager of your local grocery store.* Explain what you want to do and describe the charity sale table. Ask permission for your group to conduct an event in their store. Set a date. Ask the store to provide an empty table and a few chairs inside the entrance of the store on the day of the event. If the store is not able or willing to provide a table, you can bring your own folding table. (Our record-holding Cub Scout pack collected thousands of food items using one small card table and one small sign—but they had plenty of enthusiastic scouts!) All of this should be done long before your planned event.

If necessary, do not hesitate to contact your store on short notice. We have held charity sale tables with one day's notice when we learned a charity was running short on food. Once they understand what you're trying to accomplish, store managers tend to be supportive. It helps their community, it connects them with individuals, and of course, it sells their products!

2. *Contact your local charity in advance to see if they have flyers or brochures that can be distributed to shoppers.* Also, check to see what items are most needed. One of the best advantages of a charity sale table is that it gives groups the ability to help fill current shortages immediately.

3. *Arrange for inventory.* If your group plans to staff a charity sale table for longer than a few hours, I recommend that you preorder cases of food from the store manager one week before the event. You might collect hundreds (even thousands) of items in one day. Most stores do not have that quantity of specific items on hand. Ask the manager to order jars of peanut butter, cans of tuna, canned pasta sauce, or whatever items your

local charity needs that week. Depending on how busy your store is, calculate the number of items based on the assumption that one to two hundred items can be sold per hour. Check the lowest prices for each item that week and order that brand (typically the store brand is the lowest price without using grocery coupons).

4. *Arrive thirty to forty-five minutes before the sale is to start to set up the table*. Stock it with food items appropriate for charity that do not require coupons. Organizations should wear something to identify who they are (uniforms, T-shirts, hats, or name tags).

5. *Schedule workers*. Do not have more than six to eight students in the store at one time, or it can be disruptive to shoppers. You only need two to four students and two adults per shift (one to two hours). If you have a large group, you can staff a table all day, or staff a few stores at a time.

6. *Post a sign*. Next to items on the table, set an index card showing the price. Make a simple sign to tape on the front of the table. Our signs say:

> *"Please buy food to help _____*
> *(name of charity). Select the items and then purchase*
> *them with your grocery order."*

7. *Collect charity items*. Place items in the collection bin by the register after your purchase. Thank you, thank you, and thank you!

8. *Sell!* This is our opening line to shoppers: *"Good morning! Today we are selling food to help feed the hungry in our community. You can help for as little as 25 cents!"*

Children usually need coaching and guidance to get started, but will take over the selling process on their own as shoppers begin responding positively. If possible, explain to shoppers which charity will receive the food. Many shoppers will be unaware of a local charity in their area and may be surprised that the charity experiences food shortages. Charity sale tables are effective at raising awareness of hunger in our immediate areas. Be sure to tell shoppers to take the item from the sale table, purchase it with their order, and put the item(s) in the collection bin by the registers. If your store does not have a food collection bin for charity on hand, it is easy and effective to use a shopping cart as a collection bin with a sign made by the volunteers.

9. *Show shoppers what to do.* Some shoppers will think they need to purchase the item at your table; simply review the directions explained above to clarify the process.

10. *Delivery day!* The most wonderful part is actually delivering the groceries to the charity. You may decide to deliver the groceries as a group if the charity is open that day, or have a few children deliver them with parents after school on the following day.

Charity Sale Tables for National Hunger Awareness Day

Any group can hold a charity sale table. Go to *HungerDay.com* to print out stickers and flyers, and learn about other ideas for supporting the hunger cause. A family could staff a table for two hours, a parent could organize neighborhood children to staff a table, or a scout group could staff the event as a summer service project.

Passing the Torch

I'll never forget going on a shopping trip one Saturday morning a few years ago. I walked in the store, and a cute, smiling, ten-year-old girl asked, "Would you like to buy food for charity to help us cut out hunger today?"

To that point, I had been involved in arranging most of the charity sale tables in my area, and was working to encourage others to organize events as well. I had never stumbled upon one in action without any effort on my part.

I looked up at their colorful sign, which had the exact words suggested on the website, and even had a colorful reproduction of our logo at the top of the sign. Several smiling children stood next to the table.

You know what happened. I couldn't help it; I had to rave to those children how wonderful they were, how happy they had made me, and what a great job they were doing. At this point I think they were beginning to regret they had approached me. I'm sure other shoppers had responded nicely, but not as exuberantly.

I said, "I am the Cut Out Hunger lady! You girls are the first ones who have ever done this on your own! Of course, I'll buy food to help Cut Out Hunger!"

Since then, hundreds of children have participated in Cut Out Hunger charity sales tables without my involvement. They have no idea who the Cut Out Hunger lady is, and that's wonderful. They are "cutting out hunger" where they live and tackling their own zip codes.

You can be sure that if I stumble upon your charity sale table one day, I will probably act the same way. And I'll definitely buy food for your cause!

Girl Scouts Cut Out Hunger

Although I was thrilled with the success I had seen in my suburb, I knew I couldn't expand the program to its potential on my own. After seeing some Girl Scout leaders' success in raising food with their troops, I met with the community outreach manager at the Girl Scout Council of Northwest Georgia. I shared the concept of the Kids Cut Out Hunger program with her and asked if she saw any opportunities to incorporate Cut Out Hunger into the Girl Scouts' program.

She agreed that the program had potential to increase their already active support of the hunger cause, and arranged a "pilot test" with Girl Scouts in one suburb. After the success of that "test," the Girl Scout Council leaders and a large grocery chain organized the first "Cut Out Hunger Day" on September 16, 2003, for the benefit of the city's food bank. On that day, six hundred Girl Scouts staffed fifty-eight grocery stores on a Saturday, selling food for charity. They sold over twenty-five thousand items in one day, enough to help seventeen hundred families. They repeated the program on September 25, 2004, with equal success.

It is my hope that other Girl and Boy Scout Councils, and other youth organizations across the country, will be able to give the Kids Cut Out Hunger a try where they live.

"Kids Cut Out Hunger" Lesson Plan for Teachers

If you are interested in teaching a group of students how to use the Cut Out Hunger program, these guidelines can help you get started. Realistically students as young as nine-years old can follow this lesson plan, with some assistance from their parents, teacher, or adult leader. The elements of this lesson are appropriate for grades three through nine.

1. Ask students to save the grocery coupon circulars from their Sunday newspapers for one to two weeks prior to the lesson. Ask them to write Sunday's date on the front of the circulars and then bring them to class.

2. During the week of the lesson, go to the Best-Deals List for your store at *CouponMom.com* and print the list. Make one copy for each student.

3. At the beginning of the lesson, teach the students how to read the list, explaining each column.

4. Have students identify which items indicate they would be a good choice for "charity" and explain why these are good items for that purpose.

5. Have each student create a "charity shopping list" by looking for items that have their coupon circular date in the first column or charity items that do not have a coupon noted. If there is no date in the coupon column, that indicates the item is a good deal without having to use a coupon.

6. Have students write down the item names and final prices (after the coupon is deducted) on a sheet of paper and add up the total price for all of the items. You can also determine a spending goal in advance and have the students select items that meet that goal.

7. Have the students find and cut out the coupons for the items they have listed by looking in the grocery coupon circular that matches the circular date on the list. They can keep their coupons and list together in an envelope to take on their shopping trip.

8. If students are purchasing the items during an actual shopping trip, find out if the store offers a discount card. Young children really like getting their own store card!

9. Optional idea: Have students buy the items with their parents and bring them back to class so they can visually understand how everyone's small contribution really adds up.

10. Alternatively, arrange for students to meet at the grocery store as a group. Each student buys his or her items, and then all the items are combined in one shopping cart. Many grocery-store managers welcome school field trips and may even arrange special activities or tours for the students as part of their shopping trip.

Have students create their shopping lists. Show them these column headings on a chalkboard, or create a table like this in a document and print copies for the children. A printable worksheet is located in the Kids Program section on my website.

Here is an example of a worksheet format to use with children in planning a Cut Out Hunger shopping list:

Item	Sale Price	Coupon Face Value	Coupon Value if Doubled	Final Price Per Item	Items Required	Final Price of All Items
Tomato Sauce	$.50	$.25	$.50	Free	1	Free
Peanut Butter	$1.50	$.35	$.70	$.80	1	$.80
Chunky Soup	$1.25	$.50/2	$1/2	$.75	2	$1.50
Cereal	$1.50	$.70	$.70	$.80	1	$.80
Total Cost	$4.75				5	$3.10

In this example, the store doubles coupons up to 50 cents. Coupons over 50 cents are deducted at face value. All items listed are appropriate for charity, as they are non-perishable, nutritious items. The student is able to stay within his or her budget of $3.50 and donate five items. This individual donation is enough to provide quite a few meals, as well as much-needed protein sources.

Start Small

Cut Out Hunger is a natural with children and is enthusiastically embraced across the country by kids of all ages. However, I believe it is only fair to save you time by sharing what does not work well.

For instance, it is not a good idea to take eighty six-year-olds to the grocery store for a field trip at the same time. If you are wondering why, you can read my next book, *How to Get Other Shoppers to Hate You in Less Than Three Minutes!*

I know this because we took eighty kindergartners to our local grocery store for a shopping trip. After we explained to the students that they were not each getting their own shopping cart, we were able to teach them to remind their parents to buy one item a week for charity when they went shopping with their parent over the summer.

To make it easy to remember, we specifically suggested that they ask their parent to buy one can of tuna each week. We showed them where the tuna section was, showed them the price tags and how to find the best deal, and emphasized that even though children should not nag their parents to buy extra things at the grocery store, it is okay to nag their parents to buy one item for charity each week.

Over that summer, the Cut Out Hunger collection bin filled up faster than it ever had, feeding hundreds of people all summer. And what do you think was the most common item donated to the bin? You guessed it—tuna!

A friend of mine laughed as she told me that her son would run directly to the tuna aisle as soon as they walked in the store, which was in the middle of the store and didn't follow her list. But he got her to buy the tuna, and that's what we hoped. I could tell she was pleased that her son put the emphasis on what they were going to buy for someone else, rather than for himself.

In spite of the problems with taking so many kindergartners to a store together, the message got through. Still, my suggestion: do take children on field trips to the grocery store—but take them in smaller groups.

Chapter 13

You Can Make a Difference

When I first began my campaign to teach people how to buy food for charity, I was extremely enthusiastic. I wrote letters, called people on the phone, and met with many community leaders to enlist their support of the concept.

One minister thought my vision of flooding the food pantries was unrealistic, and said, "Remember, Stephanie, you will never be able to fill the need."

I appreciated his perspective, because the reality is no one individual can possibly wipe out hunger. However, I have come to view the hunger issue differently. Rather than getting bogged down or discouraged by the magnitude of the hunger issue, I picture real people—one person at a time.

I don't think of "one in five children in the United States" being hungry, I think of one child being hungry. Specifically, imagine if you were in a large auditorium filled with people, and one child sat crying in the corner. Of course, you'd go up to that child and ask him what was wrong. If he looked up at you and said he was crying because he was hungry, that he hadn't eaten a real meal in days, you would stop what you were doing and go buy him something to eat! No one could turn away from such a child.

I think of single mothers. You see, I am the mother of two children, with a husband who provides for us. I do not have to worry about going to work to support my family. If a child is sick, it does not disrupt my husband's job, because I stay home. That is my job. We have insurance for medicine and doctor's visits. We have enough money to pay our bills each month. We share the responsibilities of our family.

The single mother, in contrast, is responsible for everything. She has to work full-time, pay all the bills, make sure her kids are meeting their responsibilities at school, and shuttle them to sports and activities after school and on weekends. Evenings and weekends are filled with shopping, housework, and laundry. In the best of circumstances, she is able to make ends meet but is always working, with no time to relax.

When her child is sick, she has to call in to work and take a day off—or several days—perhaps without pay. Her child may require a doctor's visit or medicine that she may not be able to afford. Her children wouldn't be able to go to day care that day but she would still have to pay for day care.

In spite of working herself to the bone, she may run out of money before the end of the month. Even doing her very best there may not be enough money for groceries.

I can't wipe out hunger, but I can do my best to make sure our local food pantry has enough nutritious food donated that she has a place to turn when she needs help. I cannot bear the idea of her being turned away or being given an inadequate amount of food.

When I buy food for charity, I think of her. When I buy a jar of peanut butter, I think of her children. These are real people we are helping. This is not a statistic or a social issue. This is a mother, a child. Our donations matter to them and should matter to us.

Giving fills me with joy. I can't explain it; you just have to do it. When you deliver food to a food pantry and feel how real the need is, you know what you are doing is making a difference. What we are doing matters.

Not long ago I was delivering a van load of food to our local food pantry from a school food drive. I rushed to finish unloading the car, busily making several trips back and forth. As I was leaving, I heard a woman say something to me and turned around to see who was speaking. I saw a woman, one of the food-pantry clients, sitting on a bench waiting for her ride. I said, "Excuse me? I didn't hear you." She replied, "I said it is a nice thing you are doing for us. Thank you." And she smiled.

I smiled back and thanked her—and told her she was welcome, that I loved to do it. Then I got in my van and cried.

In that moment, she let me know that what I am doing matters. And I hope in that moment she knew that she matters. That we are not going to let her drown, that we care about her.

We are her community and we'll keep her afloat.

Afterword

Over the past few years of working on my Cut Out Hunger project, I have written various marketing plans with specific objectives. Some of them happened, but most of them didn't.

However, what did happen with my Cut Out Hunger project was far more than I ever planned, and even more than I dreamed. It has been an incredible answer to my prayers for the project, exceeding any goal I ever wrote.

Now my goal is simple: help people save money. I don't have that written on a fancy business plan; I've just memorized it. If I can do that, then everything else will fall into place.

If you read this book because you would like to save more money, I hope it has met your goal. If you liked the ideas I shared about helping to feed hungry people, even better.

Sometimes I share with groups the personal impact of the Cut Out Hunger project on my life. Specifically, I tell them what I've learned in pursuing my "dream" and what advice I give my children about pursuing their dreams.

Looking back on the project's five years, it seems simple to me now. I tell my children to dream big, work hard, and ask for help.

Dream big. The bigger your dream, the closer you'll get to it. Many people will remind you why your dream is not realistic, why it isn't possible, or why there is no way it will work. Dream big anyway. They could be wrong, you know. And probably are.

Work hard. There really aren't any shortcuts and there are no guarantees about how long you'll have to work hard before you realize your goal. The key is enjoying the work as you go along. That's success. Make a difference as you go along, enjoying working toward the dream as much as realizing it.

Ask for help. If an organization, individual, company, or media outlet can help your cause, just ask. Don't be afraid to be told no, because you probably will be. Expect they will say no but keep asking. Remember, it only takes a few yes's to get your dream off the ground. Don't stop asking before you get enough yes's. And don't forget to ask God. I'm amazed at what he has done for me.

I would like to thank you for purchasing this book. Please know that a percentage of the profits will be used to feed the hungry. God bless you.

Stephanie Nelson
The Coupon Mom

Endnotes

Chapter 1

1. Carolina Marketing Services. *2005 Trend Report*; *www.couponinfonow.com*. July 2005.

2. News America Marketing Research. *www.newsamerica.com*. July 2005

3. Food Marketing Institute. For Consumers, *General Food Storage; www.fmi.org*. July 2005.

4. Food Marketing Institute. For Consumers, Pantry Storage; *www.fmi.org*. July 2005.

Chapter 2

1. Carolina Marketing Services. "2005 Trend Report"; *www.coupon infonow.com*. July 2005.

2. *Ibid.*

3. *Ibid.*

4. Promotional Marketing Association. *Coupon Council Research; www.couponmonth.com*. July 2005.

Chapter 3

1. Progressive Grocer Magazine, April 2004; p. 36.

Chapter 4

1. USDA Center for Nutrition Policy and Promotion: "Official USDA Food Plans: Cost of Food at Home at Four Levels (Thrifty, Low Cost, Moderate Cost and Liberal)," *www.cnpp.usda.gov.* December 2004.

Chapter 5

1. Food Marketing Institute. *Facts and Figures; www.fmi.org.* July 2005.

2. Carolina Marketing Insight's *2004 Bonus Coupon Study; www.couponinfonow.com.* July 7, 2004.

Chapter 7

1. Carolina Marketing Insight's *2004 Bonus Coupon Study; www.couponinfonow.com.* July 7, 2004.

Chapter 8

1. News America Marketing research; *www.newsamerica.com.* July 2005.

Chapter 9

1. *Good Times for Many Don't End Hard Times for Low Income Renters: Despite Economic Boom, HUD Finds Affordable Housing Crisis Deepening;* Housing and Urban Development (HUD) Report to U.S. Congress. March 2000.

2. David K. Shipler, *The Working Poor: Invisible In America* (New York: Knopf, 2004), 3.

Alternative stores - Specialty stores such as food outlets, health-food stores, drugstores and discount stores that stock some common grocery items that are generally more expensive at traditional grocery stores. Also referred to as non-traditional stores.

Baby club - A program that offers bonus rewards on baby products based on qualified spending.

Best Deals List - Weekly listing of sale items matched with available coupons for specific grocery stores. Found at *CouponMom.com*.

Best-if-used-by (or before) date - A date applied to a product by the manufacturer to show when the item is beyond its best flavor or quality.

BOGO - Acronym for "Buy One, Get One Free." Other common acronyms include B1G1 or B1G1F.

Brand flexibility - Trying a competitor's brand of products.

Brand loyalty - Staying loyal to a particular brand regardless of price.

Catalina coupons - Coupons typically generated at check-out for specific items or cash-off a shopper's next order.

Charity sale table - A place where items are displayed for shoppers to purchase for area food banks and charities.

Charity shopping - Purchasing items that are appropriate for donation. These items are noted with the word 'CHARITY' on the Best-Deals List at *CouponMom.com*.

Closed (or coded) dates - Packing numbers that are used by manufacturers in tracking their products. This enables manufacturers to rotate their stock as well as locate their products in the event of a recall.

Conventional Supermarket - the original supermarket format offering a full line of groceries including meat, produce, dairy, bakery, and cleaning supplies. These stores typically carry more than 15,000 items.

Coupon limits - Store policies that dictate the number of coupons the store will double per order.

Cut Out Hunger - A national program developed to help the average shopper buy food for charity with coupons.

Discount cards - (Also called loyalty cards.) Free membership cards offered by stores for shoppers to use in order to receive special discounts and offers.

Discount merchandiser - Stores such as Wal-Mart and Target that stock personal-care, cleaning and paper products at extremely low prices compared to traditional supermarkets.

Double coupons - A store policy that matches the face value of grocery coupons (effectively doubling their value) to attract more coupon shoppers to their store.

Electronic coupons - Automatic discounts tied to the use of a store discount card. Promotional programs with specific purchase requirements trigger electronic discounts. Details of automatic promotions are typically found in the store's weekly ad circular or on signs posted near the qualifying products.

Everyday-Low-Price store - A store whose regular prices are lower than a supermarket's regular prices, advertising consistently low prices (Super Wal-Mart).

Expired dates - A date stamped on a food product by the manufacturer.

Food bank - A central warehouse and distribution system for local food pantries, charities and feeding programs. Houses and obtains food supplies to distribute to food pantry clients. *SecondHarvest.org* lists food banks throughout the United States.

Food pantry - A community organization that distributes food to those in need via food pantries in local charities and places of worship.

Food-collection bins - Containers located near or at store exits collect donations purchased by shoppers.

Free-standing insert - The official term for the grocery coupon circulars found in the Sunday newspaper.

Grocery rebate credit card - A credit card that gives its user a portion of the cost of groceries purchased.

High-impact items - Products that are purchased regularly.

High-Low-Price store - A traditional supermarket that promotes sales, deep discounts and specials to attract shoppers (Albertsons, Kroger, Safeway).

Kids Cut Out Hunger - Age-appropriate information for getting kids involved in the Cut Out Hunger program.

Loss Leader - A deeply discounted grocery sale item. The sale price is frequently lower than the store's cost for the item, but loss leaders attract shoppers.

Loyalty cards - (Also called discount cards.) Membership cards offered by retailers (free to shoppers) that give sale prices and double coupon promotions to shoppers who use a loyalty card.

Manufacturer's coupon - Coupons issued by food manufacturers, typically found in the Sunday newspaper coupon circulars.

Multiple-purchase pricing promotions - Prices of items are discounted when purchased in multiples.

National Coupon Month - A program of the Promotional Marketing Association Educational Foundation, Inc. Focuses on the benefits and celebrates the many ways consumers can save money using coupons. September; *CouponMonth.com*.

National Hunger Awareness Day - A grassroots movement to raise awareness about solving the problem of Hunger in America. Typically held in early June; *HungerDay.org*.

Printable coupon - Coupons that can be printed on your home computer from an Internet website.

Proof-of-purchase - Product packaging featuring codes and seals that shoppers use when utilizing rebate and promotional offers.

Quality guarantee - An assurance offered by stores that encourages buyers to "try it, or get the national brand free" on their store-brand items.

Rain check - A piece of paper issued by a grocery store indicating the current sales price on an item that is currently out of stock. A shopper can use the rain check in the future when the item is re-stocked.

Rebate - An offer for money-back on an item that is purchased. Stores and manufacturers sponsor instant and mail-in rebate offers.

Red-shelf boxes - Sponsored by SmartSource, these boxes are located next to featured products in a store's aisle.

Second Harvest - The nation's largest charitable hunger-relief organization with a network of more than 200 food banks across the United States, the District of Columbia and Puerto Rico. Each year the network provides assistance to more than 23 million people.

Sell-by date - A date applied to a product that tells how long the store is to display and sell the product.

Service store - A store that appeals to shoppers who are less motivated by price, focusing on high-quality products and expanded product selection (an example: Whole Foods).

Shopper reward program - A program (*Upromise.com*) that credits member-shoppers who purchase participating products.

SmartSource - The brand name of one of the two coupon companies that publishes the Sunday newspaper coupon inserts (a division of NewsAmerica Marketing).

Stocking up - Purchasing multiple amounts of products on sale.

Store brands - A store-name counterpart to a brand-name product. Many store-brand items are produced by the companies that manufacture brand-name items.

Store coupons - Coupons issued by specific retailers or grocery stores, typically found in weekly ad circulars, store magazines or in-store flyers.

Store sale cycles - Typically a product's sale cycle is two to three months.

Store savings programs - A grocery store's promotional programs, marketing strategies, and membership benefits that shoppers can use to save money at their store.

Strategic Shopping - The method in which shoppers can save money at the grocery store by changing the way they buy the foods they like. Strategic shoppers know their grocery prices, know their store's savings programs, and know their grocery coupons.

Supercenters - A large food/drug combination store and mass merchandiser under a single roof. These stores offer a variety of food as well as non-food merchandise (Wal-Mart, Kmart, Super Target, Meijer, Fred Meyer).

Superstore - A larger version of the conventional supermarket offering an expanded selection of non-food items. These stores carry about 25,000 items.

Triple coupons - A store policy that triples the face value of grocery coupons to attract more coupon shoppers.

Use-by date - The last date recommended for the use of the product while at peak quality. Date is determined by manufacturer.

Valassis - The brand name of one of two coupon companies that publishes the Sunday newspaper coupon inserts.

Virtual Coupon Organizer - An online database of coupons from the Sunday newspaper from the grocery coupon circulars. Found at *CouponMom.com*.

Warehouse store - A low-profit margin store offering reduced variety, lower service levels, and minimal décor, but features aggressive pricing (Food 4 Less, ALDI).

Wholesale club store - A membership retail/wholesale hybrid with a varied selection and limited variety of products presented in a warehouse environment (Sam's Club, Costco, BJ's).

A Gift for You ...

Premium Online Subscription
Debt-Proof Living Newsletter ... *FREE!*
(formerly *Cheapskate Monthly*)

Please accept a six-month online subscription to **Debt-Proof Living** (formerly *Cheapskate Monthly*) newsletter from DPL Press, Inc., with our thanks for buying this book.

Each monthly issue of **Debt-Proof Living** newsletter comes packed with motivation, inspiration, and practical information on every area of money management—all designed to empower you to get out of debt and live below your means—with dignity and style!

You will enjoy articles filled with practical information on how to save money on just about everything, inspiring Turning Point stories, reader mail, plus fabulous tips for how to save money every day ... and more!

But that's not all. With your **FREE** six-month online subscription to **Debt-Proof Living** newsletter (subscription rate is $24 for 12 months), you will have access to the entire members' area of *DebtProofLiving.com* including searchable back issues of *Cheapskate Monthly*, dozens of Discussion Groups, and more than 30 calculators including the highly acclaimed *Rapid Debt-Repayment Calculator.*

To activate your **FREE** subscription, go to this web page and follow the prompts:

www.DebtProofLiving.com/CPN6Free

We can't wait to welcome you to the DPL family!

This offer is limited to new subscriptions only. May not be used to renew a current subscription or given as a gift. Offer may be withdrawn at any time without notice.

DPL PRESS